The Money-Saving Gardener
Containers

The Money-Saving Gardener Containers

How to create a year-round container garden for less

ANYA LAUTENBACH

CONTENTS

6   Introduction

8   **CREATING A CONTAINER GARDEN**
22   **PLANTS FOR POTS**
50   **CONTAINER CARE**
62   **SPRING**
88   **SUMMER**
122   **AUTUMN**
150   **WINTER**
172   **CONTAINER PLANT PROPAGATION GUIDE**

186   Resources
187   Index
191   Acknowledgments
192   About the author

INTRODUCTION

When I was a girl, I spent my time watching my family growing their own food and flowers in pots, as well as in the garden. I have happy floral memories of sitting on our balcony on summer afternoons with my mum and granny, eating homemade cake and talking about the plants growing around us in various containers.

The climbing beans we grew in pots not only gave us fresh, healthy food, but also acted as a screen on the balcony, which in summer felt like a beautiful jungle. In the winter, we celebrated our pots of amaryllis blooms, giving them pride of place on the table in the sitting room for everyone to admire. They were truly our pots of joy in the darkest days of the year.

From a very early age I was taught to find joy in the simple things and potted plants always played a big role, bringing me closer to the natural world and allowing me to live a happier, more purposeful, and fulfilled life. Later, when I left home and went travelling, the garden came with me in pots. Initially, I was living in flats and shared accommodation, but this didn't stop me growing my precious green friends. Places were changing, people were coming and going, but one thing stayed the same – I always had some plants on my windowsills making me feel like I was home and that I belonged. A feeling of not belonging can be very typical for people like me with ADHD and this can be unsettling, but plants growing in containers help me to feel like I'm with my family and not alone.

I now want to share the skills I've learnt with as many people as possible and continue the legacy of those close to me, who are now gone. My mission is to show you how to create amazing displays of potted plants, no matter the size or location of your outdoor space or your budget, to bring you happiness every day of the year. Pots are like little gardens that anyone can own, and seeing people's balconies filled with various pots, often repurposed and with imperfections, as well as displays on steps, walls, and other unexpected places, always makes me smile.

Gardening in pots makes growing more flexible, too. Container growing is often possible for people who cannot raise plants in the garden, maybe due to mobility issues or because they live in temporary accommodation. Pots can also be located in the most suitable places for the plants' needs, and taken with you when you move home. They allow us to get closer to our plants, too; I often lift some of my smaller pots of flowers to admire their precious little faces or inhale their wonderful scent.

I feel a very special connection with everyone I come across through my social media channels and through my books, and I hope this one will inspire you. While it's a practical book, I've added a big part of my heart and soul into it, and I hope it will help you create dreamy pots, without spending much money. I also hope that your pots of joy will give you a sense of achievement and purpose, just as they do for me, and help you create something meaningful and long lasting.

CHAPTER 1
CREATING A CONTAINER GARDEN

As a money-saving gardener, I am always on the look-out for a bargain, and when creating a display for my patio, that starts with sourcing the containers. Here, I explain how you can find inexpensive, recycled, and pre-loved pots, and the sizes and types that suit different plants. I also show you how to arrange your containers to create beautiful effects.

CHOOSING CONTAINERS

Before you start planting any container, take a moment to consider what type of pot you need for the job, and how you can save money. Look on Pinterest and other online platforms and take pictures when visiting gardens for inspiration, as well as looking around your own garden or home for items that could make beautiful planters.

You can use almost any vessel you have at home that's reasonably waterproof as a planter – my patio is packed with all sorts, from old terracotta pots I've been given, to ceramic vases found in charity shops, and old pots and pans from the kitchen. Wooden boxes and wicker baskets are other options, although they may only last a few years before they begin to deteriorate. However, wood and wicker are both biodegradable and you can then break them up and add them to the compost heap, if you have one in your garden.

One very important factor to bear in mind is that all outdoor planters must have drainage holes in the bottom to prevent waterlogging, which will kill your plants very quickly – unless they are aquatics, of course. If your pots don't have holes, it's easy to drill a few with an electric drill and appropriate drill bit for the material you are working with, and I have transformed many of mine in this way.

Finding money-saving pots

Buying new pots can be expensive, particularly if you are in need of a large container for a shrub or tree, for example. So, how can you save money and still create a beautiful display? I've found many large pots being given away for free on local recycling websites, or you can ask around locally if anyone is downsizing and has containers to give away. Friends and family may also have unused pots or other items to spare, and reclamation yards are good sources of second-hand pots, particularly large galvanized containers. Search "salvage and reclamation near me" online to locate those close to home.

Reusing pots

I try to reuse the pots I already have at home, rather than buying new. While plastic containers may not be the best environmental or aesthetic choices, they are cheap and readily available. Like me, you may have lots of plastic plant pots from garden centres that you can reuse, or try old buckets, which can be used as larger containers that would otherwise be very expensive. These less attractive pots can be tucked behind others or in the middle of a display where you will only see the plants and flowers they are holding.

Other items that make suitable planters include recycled shoes and boots, hessian or leather shopping bags and handbags, tin cans, old toolboxes, wooden crates, cake tins, pallets, toy trucks, and even old wooden drawers or tin bathtubs, if you're creating a large display. Have fun, experiment, and see what works for you. Even broken pots can also be utilized

Right | I picked up these terracotta pots from car boot sales, which offer great bargains.

Clockwise from top left: Making seed pots from old newspaper, parcel packaging, or magazines is cheap and easy; select a container that will allow some room for root growth; an old kettle hung up at an angle to allow water to drain out makes a beautiful container for a drought-tolerant *Dichondra*; choose pots with wide brims and narrow bases for long-term plantings.

for succulents such as sedums and houseleeks (*Sempervivum*), which will thrive in a little compost tucked into a damaged container.

Don't dismiss unusual and quirky pots, since what initially might seem unsuitable for growing plants will more often than not find its match made in heaven. Just make sure you drill a few holes in the base for drainage.

I also never give up on a pot if it looks a little dirty or past its best. Try scrubbing it gently with warm water and a mild detergent to remove dirt, or leave those with algae and mosses growing on them, which lends a beautiful, timeless, weathered look.

Make your own

One of the easiest ways to save money is to grow your plants from seed, which, of course, need pots to accommodate them. I make my own little biodegradable pots from newspaper or old magazines, and from toilet paper inner rolls, all of which are biodegradable and will rot down when you plant the whole package of pot and seedlings into compost or soil, adding a few nutrients into the bargain.

To make a pot from newspaper or magazines, simply wrap a few sheets around a small jam jar or bottle, tuck the ends under to make the base, before slipping it off its mould. I find packing them together in a seed tray helps them to keep their shape. Another option is to use a manual soil block maker. This little device is a great investment, and compresses potting compost into the block shapes that allow you to grow seedlings without the need for any pots at all.

Size matters

The size of the pot you will need depends on a few factors. It must, of course, accommodate your chosen plants' roots. Plants with long roots, such as sweet peas, grow better in deep pots, while others with small root systems, such as succulents, will be happy growing in shallow containers. When propagating it's good to have a mix of sizes, including small pots and trays to sow seeds and plant cuttings, and larger containers to house seedlings and rooted stems as they grow.

Another factor to think about is the maintenance your container display will require and how much time you have to care for it. Small pots made from porous materials such as terracotta contain low volumes of compost and not much water, which means they dry out quickly, and may need watering every day in summer if planted with thirsty bedding plants. However, little pots can look wonderful when filled with drought-tolerant succulents and placed on a garden table or a chair. These compact containers can also be useful in the cooler seasons for spring bulbs, which require less water and flower when rainfall is higher and evaporation rates are low. Many people don't see potential in their shallow pots and give them away, so you'll often find them in charity shops and recycling centres.

Larger pots that contain more compost and water tend to be easier to care for, and will need watering less frequently, whatever the season (see also p.54 on watering). Then there are plants, such as agapanthus, that prefer to have their roots restrained, and will happily grow in a medium-sized pot for years.

Shaping up

For short-term displays of spring bulbs or summer bedding, any shape of container will suffice, but if you're planting trees, shrubs, or large perennial plants that will develop sizeable root systems over time, you will need a pot with a wide brim that narrows towards the base. An urn or container with a narrow neck and wide base will not be a good choice, since you won't be able to remove them when they outgrow the pot, without breaking the vessel or slicing up the root ball. This may result in you losing the container or the plant, or possibly both.

Hanging baskets

Many people like hanging baskets, and I can see their allure, but I'm not a fan of those with open, cage-like designs. These are very difficult to maintain, since water runs straight through them, and plants become dehydrated in record time in high summer. If you want a hanging display, opt for containers with solid or basketweave sides that hold moisture for longer (see project on pp.112–3).

Material choices

You will find containers made from almost every material you can imagine, from concrete, clay, and wood to metal, rattan, and plastic. Each has its pros and cons, so think about how you are going to use your planters, how long they need to last, and where you are going to site them, which may have an impact on how they weather. For example, a porous terracotta pot will quickly develop a patina of algae and mosses in a cool, damp corner, but should retain its original colour better in sun, where these organisms are less likely to thrive.

Many people start their gardening journey with a few terracotta pots, but soon find out that after a cold, frosty winter, they crack and break. My advice is to buy those labelled "frostproof", rather than "frost resistant". While they may be more expensive initially, they should last for many years – some may even have a guarantee – saving you money in the long run. Glazed containers may also break during icy weather but, in my experience, they last longer than plain frost-resistant terracotta. You can also turn empty pots or those housing perennials on their sides in winter, so water doesn't collect in them, which can help to prevent breakages during frosty conditions.

Other long-lasting containers include those made from metals, such as copper, which takes on a beautiful blue-green patina as it oxidizes; galvanized zinc and steel, with their silver or grey appearance; and powder-coated metal containers, which come in a wide range of colours. While metal is durable, it can get very hot in summer, drying out the compost and potentially scorching plant roots, so if you want to use it on a sunny patio, pair your pot with heat- and drought-tolerant plants.

Stone containers are unlikely to break, and complement a period house. However, they are heavy, difficult to move, and, when new, they tend to be quite expensive. Concrete or composite look-alikes are cheaper but the manufacture of concrete is very polluting, releasing high volumes of carbon dioxide (CO_2) into the atmosphere, and for this reason I personally try to avoid it. Plastic is also polluting, but I prefer to recycle what I have, rather than sending it to landfill.

Containers made from wood, rattan, and bamboo are good options for short-term displays, but wet conditions often cause these biodegradable materials to rot within a few years. Lining them with reused compost bags can help to prolong their life.

Right Pre-loved containers I found in second-hand shops, and paper cups, collected after a child's party, housing my seedlings.

DESIGNING A CONTAINER DISPLAY

When choosing pots and plants to form a display, think about the height, colour, and texture of both to get the best from your arrangements and create an eye-catching show all year round.

Containers are very useful for introducing colour and interest to otherwise ungardened areas, such as windowsills, patios, and seating areas, and allow you to grow plants best not grown in the ground, such as mint or bamboo, which spread rapidly.

I like to place my pots by the front door so that when I come home I'm greeted by positivity, the plants making me take a moment to pause and enjoy them. I also surround seating areas with containers, which encourage me to be mindful and look more closely at the leaves and flowers. If you place a chair among an arrangement of pots, it feels like sitting in the middle of a fragrant and beautiful border. You almost feel like part of the garden and there's so much to take in – the colours, scents, and textures bringing you closer to nature.

Basic principles

I like to think of my pot displays as little gardens, combining different shapes and colours to create a beautiful arrangement. The design principles are the same as for a border. Position large containers and plants at the back and small pots of ground-huggers at the front, but to recreate a natural look, avoid placing them in a straight line. You can even raise pots up to create a staggered and more dynamic effect, while also making them more accessible. If some pots are less attractive than others, hide them behind the prettier ones, and remember that you have the flexibility to rearrange displays, bringing plants forward when they look their best.

Designing with plants

As well as thinking about where to position your pots, it's important to consider which combinations of plants to feature in your display. Do the heights, colours, and textures work aesthetically together? Is there enough interest throughout each season? I usually stick to two or three colours in any combination, which helps to create a co-ordinated display. Try making a note of the colours and shapes you like and browse the plants I have recommended in the seasonal chapters (see pp.62–171) to match your containers.

You may also find it useful to look at a colour wheel when choosing plant combinations – colours next to each other on the wheel create an harmonious look, while hues that sit opposite one another will produce a more dynamic display.

As well as considering colours, also think about the forms and shapes of your plants. A simple way to create a balanced display is to use the "thriller, filler, spiller" principle. The thriller is the focal point of the display – usually the tallest or most dramatic plant planted in the centre of the container. Fillers are lower-growing plants that create a cushion of flowers and foliage around the thriller, while spillers are trailing plants that flow over the sides, softening the edges of the pot.

Container colours

If you follow me on social media you will know that I love colour. I'm like a magpie when I'm out and about, snooping around local charity shops in search of unusual containers, and snapping up any bargains that catch my eye. As a result, I have pots of every colour and shade, some plain, some patterned, just waiting for their perfect plant partner. While I recommend being adventurous and going for any pot or plant you like, in my experience too many rich shades in one display can fight one another, whereas a cooling complementary hue will allow the colourful star performers to shine more brightly. For example, try vibrant flowers in a simple clay or white-glazed pot, and pale colours in darker containers. Or, if you have a colourful or patterned container you want to show off, opt for a green leafy plant or white blooms.

Styles and themes

Think about your container displays as you would the interior design of your home, selecting plants and pots that reflect your personal taste, while also taking into account the style of your house and garden. For example, a group of modern containers will work well in a contemporary, urban setting, but probably won't look quite right in an old country garden.

If, like me, you have an eclectic assortment of containers, you could sort them by colour, style or material and pair them with plants to create a series of mini displays. Alternatively, group them to create a theme, such as Mediterranean, minimalist, or cottage garden, and look at Instagram and Pinterest for inspiration. Or, simply go with the flow, and see where your imagination takes you.

You can conjure up visions of a happy holiday in the sun, using Mediterranean plants such as lavender, salvias, and agapanthus that bring back memories, or involve your children to create an outdoor playroom of plants in toy trucks, prams, or wheelbarrows. Alternatively, try a potager display, mixing flowers, herbs, and edibles in pots; or a romantic cottage garden, brimming with roses, sweet peas (*Lathyrus odoratus*), and marigolds in rustic clay and wooden containers. In winter, you could even put together a Christmas-themed display with a conifer tree (see pp.162–3), and pots of berried plants and ivies.

This display of sun-lovers receives about eight to ten hours of sunlight each day in summer, and the succulents in the shallow pots at the front need very little water to thrive.

SITING YOUR POTS

Having collected together your plants and pots, it's time to think about the best spot to place them. Those with a balcony or small terrace can maximize their space by selecting their pots and plants carefully to create impact. Gardeners with a bigger plot have more options, but for all, there are useful tips to consider before setting out your store.

When siting a container display, check that the light levels your chosen area receives suit the plants you want to display. Some plants like to bask in full sun, which means that on a summer's day they are in direct sunlight for six hours or more. Those from warm climes, such as lavender, rosemary, and hebes, as well as many summer bedding plants, including cosmos, French marigolds, and petunias, fall into this category, and will either not flower or stretch to reach the light and become distorted in shadier conditions.

If your patio or balcony receives lower light levels, don't worry, as there are many pot plants that prefer a cooler site. For example, fuchsias, begonias, hellebores, and many leafy shrubs will be quite content here. You can also mix and match, placing plants that prefer shade behind those that like sun, but ensure that all receive some sunlight each day, as few plants are adapted to thrive in deep shade.

Also, check that pots are easy to reach, so that you can water and tend them easily. For example, a basket hung from a high hook may be inaccessible, or require you clambering on a chair and risking injury to water it.

Weighty issues

If you are gardening on a balcony, check that you do not exceed its load-bearing capacity, which in the UK should be a minimum of 40 pounds per square foot (PSF), but can vary, depending on its design and construction materials. While a few pots are unlikely to exceed this weight, it is worth checking that your balcony and balustrades are sound and in good repair. You can also use light containers, such as those made from zinc, aluminium, or plastics and other man-made materials, especially if you're planning to include trees or large shrubs, where the weight of the compost and water also needs to be factored in.

Ground control

Most hard surfaces are suitable for container displays, and permeable gravel will also allow excess water to drain into the ground and help to prevent localized flooding. Avoid placing your pots on lawns, however, as they will cut out the light and turn the grass yellow.

Soil-stained water will inevitably leak through the drainage holes in your pots and can create ring marks around containers placed directly on paved surfaces. Gently scrubbing with hot, soapy water will usually lift them, but the stains may not come out of porous paving such as sandstone. Placing pots on "feet" (see p.58) that raise them up off the ground can help, as rain or a hose will then wash away most of the soil residue. Or set them on bricks, paving slabs, or old floorboards to lift them off a more expensive surface.

CHAPTER 2

PLANTS FOR POTS

There are lots of ways to save money on your container plants, such as growing them from seed, taking cuttings from flowers in the garden, if you have one, and investing in long-term perennials, bulbs, and shrubs that will perform year after year. Here are some easy propagation techniques and plant choices to help you make beautiful displays for very little money.

MULTIPLY BY DIVISION

One of the quickest and easiest ways to save money on plants that spread in a pot or area in the garden via underground roots or bulbs is to lift and divide them every couple of years to make new plants for free. This foolproof propagation method is perfect for beginners.

I am always looking for ways to create stunning displays while keeping costs to a minimum, and propagating plants by division offers a great way to do both. Dividing plants couldn't be easier, and simply involves digging up plants from my borders or tipping them out of containers, and prising apart the root balls to make two or three plants from one.

Many plants spread via underground root systems or their bulbs form offsets, or baby bulbs, that develop next to the parent. This is why you can plant ten snowdrops one spring and have a whole bed filled with the little flowers a few years later. Perennial plants such as hostas (see pp.86–7), primulas, catmint (*Nepeta*) and sedges (*Carex*); herbs, including mint and thyme; and spring bulbs such as crocuses, grape hyacinths (*Muscari*), and daffodils (*Narcissus*), are all good contenders for this form of propagation.

How to divide perennials

The best time to divide hardy perennials is in early spring, just as new growth is emerging, or in autumn, before the plants die down for the winter. If you have a pot filled with a perennial with lots of stems shooting up from the root ball, you can simply tip it out of the container. Or look around the garden for plants you would like to include in your patio display, and dig around and under the roots to remove a clump.

Now take a knife and slice through the root ball to create two or three smaller clumps, each with some healthy roots attached to the stems. Alternatively, you may find some clumps can be prised apart with your fingers. Fill pots with peat-free multi-purpose compost and plant each of the divided sections in its own container. Make sure that the plants are at the same level as they were in the ground or in their original pot – stems buried too deeply may rot in damp compost.

Firm in the divided sections and water well. Keep your divisions in an area with sufficient light for that particular plant and leave them to grow on. You can then add them to a larger pot with others for a mixed display or plant them on their own.

DIVIDING SPRING BULBS

When dividing spring bulbs, dig them up either as the leaves and flowers emerge, in the case of snowdrops (see pp.164–5), or, for other bulbs, after the flowers and foliage have faded. Gently pull apart clumps before repotting bulbs that are firm and healthy.

Left Divide sedges such as *Carex* in autumn or spring, lifting a clump out of its pot and gently prising apart the root ball to make two plants.

EASY CUTTINGS

Cuttings provide you with lots of plants to fill your pots for free. Softwood and semi-ripe cuttings are taken in spring and summer, while roses can be propagated from hardwood cuttings in autumn and winter, after the leaves have fallen. Alternatively, try simply placing some stems in a glass of water at any time and watch the roots grow.

Barely a day goes by when I'm not taking cuttings in one form or another. Cuttings can be so meaningful and act like a comfort blanket if you bring them from an old garden to a new home, or from a friend or relative's place to your own. My garden is filled with my mother-in-law's plants, all taken from her beautiful garden, which I found very healing when she passed away.

Some cuttings are easier to take than others, but all offer plants for free, and learning a few simple techniques is a must for any money-saving gardener. There are a few ways to take cuttings, outlined below, and all you need are some healthy plants, a clean, sharp knife or pair of secateurs, and, for some, a pot or tray of cuttings compost.

Softwood and semi-ripe cuttings

Cuttings taken in spring or early summer from new plant growth are known as softwood cuttings, while those taken later in the year, when the stems have ripened and have a hard base and soft tip, are known as semi-ripe cuttings, but you can use the same simple method for both. Most herbaceous perennials and shrubs can be grown from these cuttings.

First, look for a non-flowering stem that has grown in the current year, and remove it just below a node (a bump on the stem from which a shoot will grow) or side-stem. Trim to about 15cm (6in), removing the lower leaves so that there are a few pairs remaining at the top. If the plant has large leaves, cut these in half to reduce water loss. Pop the cutting into a pot of peat-free cuttings compost or use a mix of multi-purpose compost with some handfuls of horticultural grit. Repeat, until you have a few cuttings in one container, ensuring that none are touching each other. Water and keep the cuttings in a light, frost-free place out of direct sun.

To keep my cuttings moist, I cover them with a used plastic bag propped up with sticks, but remember to remove it as soon as you see new shoots developing, to prevent disease.

After a few months, the cuttings will have developed roots, and you can then repot each one into a container of its own to grow on. Some softwood cuttings taken in spring, including herbs such as oregano, thyme, and mint will root within days, while others make take a few weeks.

Hardwood cuttings

This method, used for deciduous shrubs, climbers and roses, as well as fruit bushes, is very easy but you need patience, since they take about a year to fully develop.

From late autumn to late winter, after the leaves have fallen, remove a healthy stem that has grown that year, and trim it into sections

Clockwise from top left: Softwood cuttings are taken in spring from new shoots; hardwood cuttings, taken from late autumn to early spring, are ideal for roses and other shrubs; dahlia cuttings are easy to take when shoots first appear in spring; succulents and some houseplants can be propagated from leaf cuttings.

Cuttings can be grown on using the snail propagation method (see pp.74–7), which makes individual stems easy to remove and pot on when they have developed a strong set of roots.

15–45cm (6–18in) long. Make a sloping cut at the top and a straight cut at the base, below a bud or pair of buds. This helps you to identify the top from the bottom of the cutting.

Then add a layer of horticultural grit to the bottom of a large pot and top it up with peat-free soil-based compost. Insert each cutting so that two-thirds of the stem is buried and the pointed end, with a few buds, is above the surface. By spring, cuttings taken in autumn will have developed new roots, but it's best to leave them to grow on until the autumn to form a larger root ball and strong shoots. They will then be ready to pot up into individual containers to add to your patio displays.

Leaf cuttings

This is a great way to propagate houseplants, succulents, and begonias. A very easy method, which involves popping leaves in a shallow glass of water, is described on pp.148–9.

Another method, often used for large-leaved begonias, is to remove a leaf in spring or summer and place it on a kitchen cutting board. Turn the leaf over to reveal the veins, which on a begonia are raised and easy to see, and make a series of small cuts across each vein and about 2.5cm (1in).

Fill a seed tray with peat-free cuttings compost or use a clean, used food tray with holes punched in the base. Water lightly to dampen the compost. Then turn the leaf back on to its front and place flat on the surface. Peg it down with wire or paperclips so that that cuts are in contact with the compost. Leave in a warm, light room and keep the compost moist. After a few weeks you will see baby plants emerging from the cut veins, which you can then cut away from the parent leaf and pot on into individual containers of cuttings compost when they have a few leaves.

Basal cuttings

Ideal for dahlias, basal cuttings are taken from healthy tubers in spring, when new shoots start to emerge. You can buy dahlia tubers in spring or propagate from those you already own. Pot up your tubers in peat-free multi-purpose compost in early spring, leaving the old stem stub exposed above the surface.

Leave to grow on for a few weeks. When the tuber has produced shoots with at least three sets of leaves, using a sharp, clean knife, carefully remove one at the base. Remove the lower leaves and cut the remaining foliage in half to prevent them wilting. Pot up your stem in peat-free cuttings compost, with the leaves just above the surface. Repeat to make a few more cuttings. Water the pots and keep in a light, frost-free place until the cuttings begin to show signs of new growth. Then repot them into individual containers to grow on. Place outside when all risk of frost has passed in late spring or early summer.

Cuttings in water

I've left this, my favourite propagation method, to last. Rooting cuttings in water is just so simple, anyone can try it, and it is the method I usually try first. All you need are a few stems, trimmed just below a bud or node, then pop them into a glass of water and wait for roots to form. It really is as easy as that! Try hardy perennials and even fruit bushes, which will form roots in water after a few weeks. Once each stem has a good set of roots, pot it up in cuttings compost to grow on. If stems don't root, you've lost nothing, so experiment and see which of your plants works best.

SEEDS OF SUCCESS

If you are new to gardening, you may think that sowing container plants from seed is for the experienced gardener, but nothing could be further from the truth. There are many annual and perennial plants that grow quickly from seed and flower in the same year, delivering bountiful container displays for just a few pennies.

For those who have never grown plants from seed, you are in for a treat. Take a look at any online seed merchant's website and you will be astounded by the variety of plants on offer, from quick-growing annuals that you sow in spring for summer flowers, to perennials, some of which may take longer to germinate and grow, but will then perform year after year, once established. Seeds are a fraction of the price of more mature plants, and you may find you are able to give some of your seedlings away to friends and family, too.

How to sow seeds

Sow hardy annuals and perennials from early to mid-spring, either indoors or in a sheltered spot outside – they may take longer to germinate outside in cooler conditions and you will need to cover them with fine netting so birds and other animals don't eat them. Pull the netting taut and secure it well, so that birds don't get tangled in it.

Some annuals, such as sweet peas, can be sown in autumn and overwintered outside on a sheltered patio (see pp.134–5). They will then flower earlier the following summer than those sown in spring. Tender or half-hardy annuals, such as petunias and French marigolds, must be kept indoors, in a sheltered area next to a sunny house wall, or in an unheated porch, until the frosts have passed.

Before sowing, fill pots or trays with damp seed compost and gently press it down with a glass to remove any large air gaps. Check the seed packet to see how deep your chosen variety should be sown – those that need light to germinate are sown on the surface, while larger seeds such as sunflowers should be buried a little deeper. Sow thinly so that the resulting seedlings are not too cramped.

Place an old transparent plastic bag over the pot or tray, and prop it up around the edges with small sticks such as cocktail sticks. This helps to keep the warmth and moisture in, but the bag must be removed as soon as the seedlings emerge to prevent fungal diseases.

When the seedlings have a couple of sets of leaves, hold a leaf and use a teaspoon or a small, sharp stick from the garden to carefully lift the root ball out of the compost and transplant it to a pot or module of its own. Leave to grow on, repotting the seedling into larger containers as they grow.

Fast-germinating seeds

For impatient gardeners, try fast-germinating seeds that are easy to grow, such as cosmos, nasturtiums (*Tropaeolum majus*), sunflowers (*Helianthus annuus*), and zinnias, which germinate within two weeks. You will find a host of different colours and varieties from seed merchants to make your pots zing.

Sowing seeds is one of the cheapest and easiest ways to fill your containers with flowers and foliage throughout the year. Summer flowers are sown in autumn or spring; sow those that bloom in autumn and winter from early to midsummer.

Clockwise from top left: Once you have a few forget-me-nots in the garden, you will never be without some free seedlings to dress up your pots each spring; *Verbena bonariensis* is another beautiful self-sower; honeywort (*Cerinthe major*) has pretty, purple, tubular flowers and distributes its seeds widely in my garden; mallows are also super self-seeders and make lovely plants for large pots.

SELF-SOWN GEMS

One of my favourite pastimes in spring is wandering around the garden on a seedling hunt. Many plants self-seed and you will find new life popping up in your beds and borders, in your patio pots and even in a gravel driveway. Familiarizing yourself with these baby plants pays dividends, providing you with more flowers for free.

Forget-me-nots, aquilegias, verbenas, salvias, ornamental grasses, and even lavender are just some of the gems I have found growing unaided in the garden from spring to autumn. As a money-saving gardener, this is manna from heaven, delivering free displays of flowers with the minimum of effort from me.

Free collection

The trick is to learn what plants look like at the seedling stage, so that you can identify them and check that they are not weeds. If I am unsure of whether a seedling is worth keeping, I use my phone to identify it, or take a quick snap and check what other plants nearby look like at this stage of growth, as some can appear a little different from their parents, before the leaves mature.

Even if you don't have a garden with beds and borders to explore, you may find that your potted plants are self-seeding into other containers or the cracks between the paving in a patio. Grasses and the tall *Verbena bonariensis*, as well as the lovely little daisy-like Mexican fleabane (*Erigeron karvinskianus*) are apt to seed into my paved areas, the sandy conditions providing ideal germination sites for them.

Before you set off on your seedling hunt, put a trowel in your pocket and set a few pots filled with moist peat-free compost in a tray, so that you can transfer your treasures quickly, before their roots become dehydrated and the plants start to wilt. Once rehomed into individual pots, I find these seedlings put on growth very quickly, but do keep an eye on them and water when the top of the compost feels dry. Their new pots must also have drainage holes, as many of these self-seeders will balk at wet soil conditions.

Autumn stars

You will find seedlings of later flowering plants and biennials (plants that produce leaves in their first year and flowers in the second) popping up throughout the summer and autumn in your borders. While many will overwinter, I like to give them the best chance of survival by digging them up as soon as I find them, so that other plants won't shade them out, which is always a risk at this time of year. If you spot some in summer and are going on holiday, leave them in the ground until you return. Those to look out for later in the year include gaura (*Oenothera lindheimeri*), forget-me-nots (*Myosotis sylvatica*), hardy geraniums, wallflowers (*Erysimum*), astrantias, and foxgloves (*Digitalis purpurea*).

Some perennials may need to be nurtured for up to a year or more before they bloom, so check the identity of what you have found and make sure you have the space and time to look after them.

LONG-LASTING SHRUBS

Shrubs may not be the cheapest plants to buy, and their flowers are often quite subtle, but they still represent great value-for-money in container displays. Given sufficient water and nutrients, some will perform for many years in a pot, offering beautiful leaf interest and a cool foil for brighter blooms. Many are also easy to propagate.

I like to mix and match my plants in pots and use evergreen shrubs such as camellias (see pp.78–9), skimmias, sweet box (*Sarcococca*), and *Pittosporum* as sculptural backdrops to some of my showier flowers. Their blooms, when they appear, are a bonus, too, many adding scent and pops of colour in winter and early spring before the summer flowers appear.

Pots also allow you to grow shrubs that would not normally like the soil conditions in your garden. For example, if you have chalky, alkaline soil but would like to grow acid-loving rhododendrons, azaleas, *Pieris*, or blue-flowered hydrangeas, you can plant them in large pots of ericaceous (acid) compost and keep them healthy with a fertilizer formulated for these plants.

Potted shrubs such as fuchsias and hebes can also be used to plug seasonal gaps in a border. Pop the containers into spaces left after spring bulbs or early perennials have died down, then move them back to the patio in winter to allow the border plants to regrow.

Space invaders

Many shrubs will grow into large plants when planted in the ground, but keeping them in a container can help to restrict their size. However, they will perform best when given space to expand, so select a container that is large enough for their roots to grow without repotting them every year or two. A larger vessel will hold more compost and water, too, which will help to keep your shrubs hydrated for longer between waterings. Adding a layer of gravel or wood chips over the soil surface will also help to trap moisture in the compost and reduce evaporation rates in summer.

Small but perfectly formed

While big shrubs offer architectural interest, I also like to use more compact plants as breaks between the flowers at the front of a display. My favourites include hebes, winter-flowering heathers (*Erica*), and the herbs sage and thyme. Hardy fuchsias sit somewhere between these low growers and the taller shrubs; they flower all summer and into the autumn, but will then lose their leaves over winter before growth starts again in spring.

Layering to make free shrubs

You can save money and make new shrubs (and climbers) for free by layering them. Simply fill a pot with multi-purpose compost, then select a low-growing, flexible stem on the shrub. Make a small cut halfway through the stem at a leaf joint about 30cm (12in) from the tip. Bury the wounded stem in the pot of compost, keeping it in place with wire pins. Keep the compost moist and roots will develop on the stem within 6–12 months, at which point, sever the stem from the parent plant and pot up your cutting to grow on.

Clockwise from top left: Hebes are a versatile group of plants, grown for both their foliage and pretty summer or autumn flowers; fuchsias are a great choice for containers in semi-shade and most flower all summer; I love my hydrangeas, many of which I've grown from cuttings to decorate my patio; the fragrant, spidery winter flowers of sweet box (*Sarcococca*) are prefect for a pot by the front door.

Clockwise from top left: The daisies and foliage of Mexican fleabane creates a frill of colour almost all year round on my patio, setting off seasonal flowers in front; *Carex* and other grasses offer year-round textural interest; tender succulents are dual-purpose, providing summer colour outside and winter interest indoors; tiarellas have pretty overwintering leaves and starry spring flowers.

YEAR-ROUND INTEREST

Creating a container display that offers a long season of interest is essential if you have a small space, such as a balcony, roof terrace, or windowsill, with nowhere to store plants after they have peaked. Luckily, there are many plants for pots that will stay the course and offer colour and structure all year round.

As a money-saving gardener, I like to include plants in my container displays that offer great value by providing long-lasting interest. Any plant that will sit happily in its pot for twelve months of the year, decorating my patio with evergreen foliage or flowers, followed by seedheads, gets my approval, and over the years I've experimented with a few that have become firm favourites.

There are evergreen shrubs (see pp.34–5) on that list, of course, but I also like to mix things up with other beauties that I wouldn't be without. Evergreen grasses and sedges such as stripy *Carex* species and *Festuca glauca*, with its steely blue year-round foliage; the dainty Mexican fleabane (*Erigeron karvinskianus*), with its daisy-like flowers that bloom from spring to late autumn over small evergreen leaves; heucheras and tiarellas, with their colourful foliage; and small-leaved ivies are among the best for containers.

Evolving beauties

Deciduous perennial plants can offer long-lasting interest, too. My favourites include hydrangeas, which come into leaf in spring, flower for ages from summer to early autumn, and then offer wonderful seedheads that overwinter. The cone flowers, *Rudbeckia* and *Echinacea*, and many of the asters (see p.90 and p.124) produce leafy stems early in the year, followed by late summer flowers and pretty seedheads that stand over winter.

Deciduous grasses, including *Panicum*, the tufted hairgrass (*Deschampsia cespitosa*), and dwarf varieties of *Miscanthus sinensis* are also good contenders for large pots, their foliage creating a foil for other plants in late spring and summer, while the autumn flowers and winter seedheads look dramatic in the colder months, particularly when dusted with frost (see p.128 on how to grow grasses). The annual foxtail millet (*Setaria italica*) is another wonderful grass with autumn seedheads loved by birds.

Tiny beauties

Diminutive hardy succulents, including *Sedum album* and houseleeks (*Sempervivum*), provide year-round decoration in pots outside. You can add evergreen echeverias and the paddle plant (*Kalanchoe thyrsiflora*) to the mix in summer and then bring these tender beauties indoors to decorate a windowsill or bright room from autumn to late spring.

Clockwise from top left: I grew cucumbers in a pot last year, with a twig pyramid supporting the climbing stems; blueberries are grown in pots of peat-free ericaceous compost; bush tomatoes are easy to grow in large hanging baskets; bring the taste of summer to your patio or balcony with a few containers filled with strawberry plants.

GROW YOUR OWN

My husband is a keen vegetable grower and his enthusiasm spills over to me in the summer when I like to grow a few soft fruits and tender veg such as tomatoes in pots on my sunny patio. These mingle beautifully with the flowers, delivering a feast for the eyes and the tastebuds.

Growing food in containers is easy and my boys like to raise a few vegetables on the patio, which they help to plant and reap the rewards later in the summer. Our favourites include tomatoes, peppers, and chillies in the hot spots close to the house, and fruits such as strawberries, currants, and blueberries.

Easy vegetable crops to grow in containers include lettuces, kohlrabi (see pp.136–7), courgettes, cucamelons (see pp.118–9), and even potatoes. Some will deliver just a handful of crops in a container, but exceptions include lettuces, tomatoes, chillies, and courgettes, which will produce a decent-sized harvest, if you have space for a few pots of each.

Salad leaves

Unlike most vegetables, which like a sunny site, lettuces and other salad leaves cope with some shade. I sow batches of seed from spring to late summer outside, filling trays with seed compost and sprinkling the seeds on the surface, then covering them with a fine layer of compost. Place them on bricks in trays filled with water to protect the emerging seedlings from slugs and snails. Water regularly and the leaves will be ready to harvest within a few weeks. If you opt for the cut-and-come-again varieties, you can snip off the young seedlings when they reach about 15cm (6in) in height, leaving the stubs to regrow for a second crop.

Tomatoes, chillies, and courgettes

These tender crops must only be planted outside after the frosts in late spring. Sow the seeds, following the instructions on the packs, in early spring on a windowsill indoors and transplant the seedlings when they have a few sets of leaves into their own individual pots. Finally, transfer them into larger containers and set them outside after the frosts. Choose outdoor tomatoes, and add a cane to the pot to support the stems of cordon varieties. Also remove the shoots growing between the main stem and side-stems, as they drain the plant of energy needed to produce the fruits.

Courgettes are very easy to grow but they form big plants and need large pots. Regular watering, avoiding the leaves if possible, will help to produce healthy plants and heavy crops – two plants will feed a family of four. Chillies need heat to mature so find the hottest, most sheltered spot for these jewels.

Fruity favourites

If you only have a small space to grow fruit, I would opt for strawberries (see pp.120–1). Buy runners in the autumn and pot up the baby strawberry plantlets that appear on long stems each year, to replace old plants for free. Blueberries are easy to grow in pots of ericaceous compost. Buy two plants to cross-fertilize, and feed with a fertilizer designed for acid-loving plants when the flowers appear.

CLIMBING PLANTS

Providing much-needed height to a display, climbing plants can transform your container garden with spiralling stems of flowers and foliage. You can also use them to decorate a wall or fence by adding trellis or wires to support your climbers, or allow the lax stems of ivies and *Ipomoea batatas* to trail from a tall pot or hanging basket.

Pots packed with climbers will envelop a seating area with flowers and foliage, while sweet peas will also wrap you in their wonderful fragrance.

Annual climbers, such as black-eyed Susans (*Thunbergia alata*), sweet peas, and the purple bell vine (*Rhodochiton atrosanguineus*) can be grown from seed in autumn or spring for very little money. The plants these little packages produce make a big impact, some scaling heights of up to 2.5m (8ft), so do bear this in mind if space is tight. Check heights and spreads on plant and seed labels carefully before buying to ensure you can accommodate these towering beauties.

Support system

Apart from the self-clinging climbers such as ivies, most need a support to haul themselves up to the light. The annuals and perennials such as clematis have twining stems or tendrils that wrap around their supports, while climbing roses use their thorns to hook on to trellis or other plants.

You will need to add a support of some kind for container-grown climbers, and my preference is a wigwam of sticks and stems that I create from prunings, which are, of course, free. These natural materials also blend seamlessly with the plants and soon become almost invisible beneath their leafy stems. If you don't have a garden to harvest your stems from, you can buy hazel stems in bundles (see p.186) or bamboo canes to create a wigwam.

If you want to cover a wall or fence with a climber, the cheapest and neatest option is to use horizontal wires threaded through vine eyes, which you screw into mortar between the bricks or wooden fence posts. Trellis is another option, but will cost more if new.

Big is beautiful

Climbers need space and won't perform to their full potential in a small pot, so source a large container such as a half barrel, upcycled tin bathtub, or a wooden crate. Fill with peat-free multi-purpose compost, if growing annuals, or peat-free loam-based compost for perennials such as clematis.

Sow seeds of tender climbers indoors in early spring, and plant outside when all risk of frost has passed, setting one seedling next to each of the legs of your support. You can sow sweet peas in the autumn, too (see pp.134–5), and overwinter the seedlings in a sheltered spot outside. These will then produce robust plants that flower from early summer.

You may have to tie the stems of your twining climbers to their support with soft garden twine initially, but they will then cling of their own accord as they grow, and can be left to scramble up unaided.

Clockwise from top left: I grew this pink *Thunbergia* from seed in spring to decorate a sunny wall; Clematis need big pots and trellis or a tripod to support their scrambling stems; take cuttings of sweet peas in spring to make new plants for free.

PROPAGATING SWEET PEAS

If only a few sweet peas germinate from seed, you can propagate individual stems of those that do appear when they are about 15cm (6in) in height. Snip two or three from the base of each healthy plant and pop them in a glass of water to root. I have made many new plants to boost my stocks using this method.

There's nothing like the sweet scent of hyacinths to lift your spirits in spring. I grow them in pots outside my back door for a whiff of their fragrance every time I go outside.

FRAGRANT FAVOURITES

The scent of a rose in summer or fragrance from sweet box in winter instantly lifts my mood, while research shows that the scent of rosemary can help us concentrate and reduces stress, so include a few perfumed plants on your patio to reap these benefits.

Fragrance has a powerful effect on us, and research shows that scent brings back memories more than visual images. Scientists believe this is because the area of the brain that identifies aromas has a direct connection to the amygdala, responsible for processing emotion, and the hippocampus, which aids memory. You can conjure up wonderful memories of happy times with scented plants in pots set close to a seating area or walkway, where you can enjoy them when you're outside. I have some roses that were taken from cuttings from my mother-in-law's garden that help keep me connected with the time I spent with her when she was alive.

My granny also grew some wonderful roses and would bring a bouquet of them to me on my birthday – even today, decades later, the scent of certain roses takes me back to that time. My mum also grew scented flowers and I remember summer evenings filled with the fragrance of stocks (*Matthiola longipetala* subsp. *bicornis*) and heliotropes, which I now grow on my own patio.

Seasonal scents

For the longest season of scent, include pots of fragrant plants that flower at different times. Starting in spring, I love the smell of jonquils and 'Thalia' narcissi, which bloom early in the season, and, of course, hyacinths, some of which I force into flower indoors at Christmas time, then plant in the garden to bloom again in following years. Daphnes are another favourite for early spring fragrance.

Late spring brings the scent of perfumed shrubs such as azaleas and viburnums, together with sweet Williams (*Dianthus barbatus*). These are followed in summer by roses, sweet peas (*Lathyrus odoratus*), pinks (*Dianthus*), sweet alyssum (*Lobularia maritima*), and *Nemesia* 'Wisley Vanilla', which has a delicious scent that's best appreciated at close range. Lavender is also in bloom now, and while the scent of the leaves can be appreciated all year round, the flowers really pack a punch. Many fragrant annuals flower from summer through to autumn, including tobacco plants (*Nicotiana*) that produce their scent in the evenings, and blue and purple petunias, which can be grown at nose height in a basket.

I have a few pots of sweet box (*Sarcococca confusa*) for winter scent, which often takes me by surprise as its little white flowers are quite inconspicuous and bloom just after New Year.

EXTENDING THE FLOWER SEASON

Cutting the flowering stems of annuals such as sweet peas and tobacco plants prompts the plants to make more blooms, so pick them regularly to create posies for the house to enjoy their scent indoors, too.

SHADE-LOVERS

I like to use containerized plants to brighten up gloomy corners of the garden, but plant choices can be more limited for these areas. Undeterred, I have experimented with various plants to see which work best in these shady situations.

Containers can come into their own in shady areas where plants may struggle to thrive, such as under trees where the ground is packed solid with roots, and in the darker corners of a paved patio.

While there is a wide choice of flowers for a sunny site, a surprising number will be happy in less than six hours of direct sunlight each day in summer. My favourites for pots include snowdrops, daffodils, fuchsias, tobacco plants (*Nicotiana*), violas, bergenias, busy lizzies (*Impatiens*) heucheras, primulas, and astrantias.

Add these to the many leafy shrubs that prefer a little shade, such as viburnums, rhododendrons, camellias, and hydrangeas, for a wonderful arrangement that offers year-round interest. Ferns are another great choice for pots, their lacy fronds brightening up cool, shady spots. Good choices include the copper shield fern (*Dryopteris erythrosora*), soft shield fern (*Polystichum setiferum*), and common polypody (*Polypodium vulgare*), which tolerate the drier conditions in a pot.

Shady edibles

A few edible plants that grow well in pots tolerate some shade, including lettuces and alpine strawberries, which often self-seed in the garden. The Japanese greens mizuna and mibuna also prefer cooler conditions – they can be grown as a cut-and-come-again crop, in the same way as lettuces (see p.41). For those who want to grow herbs in a shady spot, try mint, coriander, parsley, and bay (*Laurus nobilis*), which is surprisingly shade-tolerant, despite hailing from sun-drenched countries in the Mediterranean region.

Delving deeper

While many plants are happy in part shade, only a few will tolerate really deep shade – ivy (*Hedera helix*), the holly olive (*Osmanthus heterophyllus*), and *Aucuba japonica* are some of the exceptions that will brighten a dark corner. The shrubs *Osmanthus* and *Aucuba* can be bought as relatively inexpensive young plants but will need to be transplanted into bigger pots every few years as they grow.

In areas where sunlight rarely reaches ground level, you may find your choices increase by planting in tall pots that raise them up to catch more light. Also try painting your fences or walls a light colour to reflect more sun into the area, or if shade is cast by a tree or shrub, remove the lower branches to allow more light in. Planting in colourful glazed containers also adds interest to shady plantings, while adding white or brightly coloured furniture can also help to lift a gloomy patio. Buy second-hand metal or wooden chairs and tables and paint them with a suitable exterior paint in orange, yellow, pink, or whatever colour takes your fancy and will make you smile.

Clockwise from top left: *Tiarella* is a beautiful shade-loving perennial, with overwintering leaves and wands of small spring flowers; hostas' bold foliage adds drama to low-light areas: heucheras come in a wide range of leaf colours, and make a great foil for green foliage and flowers in pots.

PUSH THE BOUNDARIES

When planting in shade, be brave and experiment with a range of plants, which sometimes surprise us and do well in areas we did not expect them to grow. If the label says a plant will tolerate some shade, push the boundaries by placing it in full shade and see what happens – growing in pots means that you can always move the plant if it is unhappy. I find this is a lovely way to be mindful, to slow down, and to observe.

Taking cuttings of your pelargoniums is a quick and easy way to guarantee their survival over winter, and saves money on new plant purchases each year.

OVERWINTERING POTTED PLANTS

One easy way to save money on container plants is to keep them from year to year. Hardy types can be left outside in their pots over winter, but tender plants often need more care to get them through the colder months, although in my experience some are tougher than their labels may suggest.

Most hardy plants in pots will sail through winter unscathed, but I can't resist including some beautiful tender perennials in my summer pots, too. Often sold as bedding, they flower outside from late spring to mid-autumn and provide great value for money, since they offer such a long season of interest.

You may find these plants described online or in seed catalogues as "half-hardy perennials, often grown as annuals", and many can be sown in spring for the price of a cup of coffee. My favourites include nemesias, geraniums (*Pelargonium*), snapdragons (*Antirrhinum*), salvias, and bacopa (*Chaenostoma cordatum*). Frost-tender dahlias and begonias, which grow from tubers, also make wonderful container plants and bloom for many months.

Seeking shelter
While tender plants create beautiful container displays when the sun shines, as autumn approaches, many people assign them to the compost or green waste bin, but my advice is to think again. Plants such as nemesias, diascias, and pelargoniums will survive a few degrees below freezing, and while winter temperatures in the garden may plunge lower, those in pots are easily moved to a more sheltered spot, such as under the eaves of the house, where their chances of survival are much higher. Even in cold areas, the temperature on a sheltered windowsill outside, or next to a house wall, especially if it's south-facing, will be a few degrees higher than an exposed garden. You may also find that plants tolerate lower temperatures if their compost is kept dry over winter, as many succumb when their roots die off in cold, wet soil.

Cut to the chase
In colder areas or where you have no space to store pots outside, try taking cuttings in late summer or early autumn (see p.26) and overwinter them indoors on a windowsill. These will produce new plants for the following year at almost no additional cost.

Dahlias and begonias are also easy to store. To overwinter them, wait until the frost has blackened the foliage, then trim the stems back, and tip them out of their pots. Shake off excess compost and place them upside down to dry in a cool, frost-free place. In a clean pot or cardboard box from the supermarket lined with newspaper, add a layer of used compost, set the tubers on top, and cover them with more compost, before storing them in a frost-free spot indoors or in a garage or shed. They will then bounce back to life in spring.

CHAPTER 3
CONTAINER CARE

Having chosen your money-saving containers and plants, you now need to care for them so that the flowers and foliage you've invested in thrive and create a beautiful display. A little knowledge goes a long way in the garden, and learning how to keep your plants healthy, so that they don't need replacing frequently, is key to minimizing costs.

CHOOSING COMPOSTS

The compost you use may affect germination rates and growth, so it's worth taking a little time to discover what's best for your seedlings and plants. Some have more nutrients to boost growth, while aggregates such as grit can be used to make a compost more free-draining for drought-loving plants that may suffer in wet soil conditions.

Selecting an appropriate potting compost for your containerized plants is very important, and the first thing I would urge you to check is that the pack is clearly marked "peat-free". In the UK and Europe, peat is being phased out in garden products and plants, but in other countries around the world there is no official ban, so check carefully. The reason peat is such a hot topic is because the bogs from which it is harvested are vital carbon stores – they hold more carbon than the world's forests combined, despite covering just 3 per cent of the Earth's land surface. Peat bogs are also precious habitats for unique flora and fauna.

Composts for different stages of growth

The potting composts you buy at the garden centre are carefully formulated to suit plants at different stages of growth, and different types of plants, so it's worth checking that you pick up the right one.

Seed and cuttings compost is free-draining and has a fine texture so that small seeds can make contact with the particles. It also contains a lower level of nutrients than other composts because seeds contain most of the nutrients they need to germinate.

Multi-purpose compost is made up of organic matter, such as fine bark and wood fibre, as well as some sterilized loam and sand. Use it for mature plants such as annuals, biennials, and bedding that will stay in their containers for a year or two.

Soil-based composts, such as John Innes types, contain a higher proportion of loam than multi-purpose, although this can be variable, and they are the best choices for perennials and shrubs that will grow in their containers for more than two years. The numbers given to John Innes composts refer to the nutrient levels in each type, with No. 1 containing the lowest level and No. 3 the highest. Young plants ready to be potted on will do well in John Innes No. 1, while a richer No. 3 is best for mature perennials, shrubs, and trees. Soil-based composts also tend to be heavier and hold more water.

Which compost for what plant?

Some plants such as rhododendrons, azaleas, skimmias, and camellias prefer acid soil conditions and, when grown in pots, they will thrive in ericaceous (acid) compost. Planting these in regular multi-purpose or soil-based composts may result in yellowing leaves.

You can also buy compost for houseplants, but this is often more expensive than multi-purpose, which usually works just as well, with a little horticultural grit to make it more free-draining. However, compost for orchids is enriched with pine bark and mimics their natural growing conditions, so it may be worth the extra expense.

Succulents and plants that hail from the Mediterranean and similar climates around the world prefer free-draining composts, which you can create by adding horticultural grit to multi-purpose or a soil-based product such as John Innes No. 2 – two handfuls added to a 2-litre pot is about right.

Making your own

While it may be quite difficult to create the perfect potting compost at home, I like to stretch my bought products and save a little money by augmenting them with some of my homemade compost or leaf mould, which is easy to produce if you have some deciduous trees and shrubs in the garden. Simply pack the autumn leaves into an old compost bag and leave them to rot down in a quiet spot in the garden for a year or two.

If you are lifting a lawn to make a new flowerbed, stack the turves upside down at the back of a flowerbed or behind the shed and leave them to rot down. You can then use the composted soil and grass as a soil-based potting compost for long-term plantings such as perennials and shrubs.

I also reuse my composts. If the plants they have homed for a year or so were free of disease, there is no reason why they can't be used again, with some additional fertilizer (see p.57) to top up the nutrient content. Recycled compost is also perfect for sowing seeds or propagation, when fewer nutrients are needed.

Composts and growing media you will need for a variety of plants, including, from left to right, horticultural grit; ericaceous compost; seed and cuttings compost; multi-purpose; and soil-based John Innes compost, all formulated without peat.

WATERING AND MULCHING

Plants in pots need watering more frequently than mature plants growing in the ground, where the roots can access water reserves in the lower depths of the soil. Potted plants, on the other hand, rely solely on the water you supply, but there are some easy ways to keep your containers hydrated for longer, saving you time and money.

The main job for container gardeners in summer is watering, which can be a daily task if your pots are standing on a sunny patio. If you have little time and don't want to spend a fortune on water bills, opt for larger pots, which hold more moisture and retain it for longer than small containers.

Another tip is to apply water to the surface of the compost, rather than the leaves and flowers, ensuring the moisture reaches the roots, where it is needed. Providing enough water with each application is also important – you may need more than you think to ensure it reaches the lower depths of the pot and starts flowing out of the drainage hole at the bottom. This encourages the plants' roots to grow down to seek the moisture, whereas a light sprinkling that only wets the top layers will keep them closer to the surface, where they will be more likely to dry out. Leaving a gap of about 2.5cm (1in) between the compost and rim of the pot also allows water to accumulate here and drain down into the compost – water will spill over the sides and not wet the compost thoroughly if you fill a container to the brim.

Mulching matters

Adding a layer of material (known as mulch) such as homemade compost, gravel, or bark chips over the surface of the potting compost will help to lower evaporation rates and preserve the water levels in a pot for longer. Mulching helps to keep roots hydrated and reduces the need to water as frequently, saving you time and money, while also reducing weed growth on the surface. Use a dry mulch such as bark chips or gravel for shrubs and trees, as damp homemade compost next to the stems may rot them over time.

Harvesting water

An easy way to save money on water bills and keep your potted plants hydrated is to install a water butt to capture the rainfall from the house roof and garden outbuildings, if you have any. Butts are easy to install and come with full instructions on how to divert water from the downpipes. Remember that they need to be raised up on bricks or a stand, so that you can fit a watering can under the tap. Most mature plants and many houseplants prefer rainwater to tap water, but it may contain some contaminants from the roof that may affect the growth of seedlings, so stick to tap water for these babies.

If a storm is forecast I also put out a few empty buckets around the garden to add to my water reserves, covering the tops with chicken wire so garden creatures can't fall in. You can do this if you have a roof terrace or an exposed balcony, too.

Clockwise from top left: Target the spout of your watering can onto the compost or mulch, so water reaches the roots; mulch plants to prevent moisture evaporating from the soil; plunge smaller pots in a bucket of water to rehydrate them.

30-MINUTE DUNK

To make sure my smaller pots are thoroughly watered, I plunge them into buckets of water for 30 minutes. The pots then draw up the moisture, ensuring all the compost is saturated, after which I leave them on a permeable surface such as my gravel drive or on bricks to drain. I then don't need to water them for a few days, even at the height of summer.

Clockwise from top left: I make my potassium-rich fertilizer from comfrey; store your homemade fertilizers in large tubs with lids – they are very smelly, so a lid is essential; feed potted flowering plants every week in the growing season from late spring to early autumn; dilute plant-based fertilizer in water before applying it.

FEEDING POTTED PLANTS

All plants grown in containers will need some additional nutrients to keep them healthy. Potting composts contain some fertilizer, which usually lasts about six weeks, after which you will need to top up supplies to keep plants healthy and flowering well. Permanent plants such as perennials and shrubs also need a boost in spring.

When I've taken time to propagate and grow on my plants, I want to make sure they continue to thrive, and this is where regular feeding comes into play. To save money I make my own from plants in the garden, such as comfrey and nettles, which gives my potted displays a boost and makes a real difference to their performances.

These natural fertilizers offer low levels of nutrients that won't harm the environment, unlike many synthetic feeds, some of which contain micro-plastics and high levels of nitrogen and other chemicals that contribute to the pollution in our rivers and oceans. However, using any fertilizer to excess, including organic types or natural products, can cause pollution, so it is better to under feed than overdo it.

You can, of course, buy fertilizers and I do splash out for plants that need special treatment, such as acid-loving camellias and rhododendrons that require a formula designed to keep them healthy (see p.79). I always check that the fertilizers I buy are "organic", and made from natural plant or animal products, which also tend to be slower-acting and deliver their nutrients over a longer period. When selecting any fertilizer, I personally look for brands that are free from synthetic chemicals and animal products. My favourites are those made from seaweed, which offer a higher proportion of key plant nutrients than homemade, and are useful for hungry plants such as vegetables and fruit.

Make your own

It's very easy to make your own fertilizer from plants in the garden and it's free. I use stinging nettles, grass cuttings, and comfrey, packing the leaves of each into separate buckets and covering them with water, then adding a lid to retain any unpleasant smells and prevent wildlife from falling in. Leave the grass cuttings and nettles to infuse for about two weeks and the comfrey for six weeks, then dilute them with one part fertilizer to ten parts water before applying to your plants.

What to feed when

I start feeding permanent plants in pots, including shrubs and perennials, in spring with an organic, plant-based, nitrogen-rich fertilizer such as the one make from grass or nettles (see above). I apply this once a week.

Annuals and bedding plants will survive for a few weeks on the fertilizer in the compost, and I then apply my own homemade comfrey feed once a week. Comfrey feed is a good source of potassium, the key nutrient needed by plants to make flowers and fruit. You can also buy both types of fertilizer.

DRAINAGE AND PLANT PROTECTION

Plant containers must provide good drainage to prevent waterlogging, which can cause diseases such as root and stem rot. Protecting your plants from excessive moisture and from garden creatures such as squirrels is easy and will save precious plants from being lost.

My collection of pre-loved and repurposed containers are all shapes and sizes, but I make sure they all have drainage holes in the base to keep my plants healthy. Apart from aquatics, all plant roots need sufficient oxygen to breathe and, like us, they will drown if the soil or compost becomes waterlogged. Wet compost may also cause harmful fungal diseases, including root rot and powdery mildew, to take hold.

To avoid problems, you can drill holes in a wide range of containers to transform them into planters, and all you need is an electric drill and drill bits designed for the material, such as ceramics, metal, and terracotta.

Some experts advise adding a broken piece of clay pot or a stone over the drainage holes to prevent them clogging up, but research shows that this is not necessary. However, these items may help to prevent soil falling out of the holes, so add them if you wish.

Feet up

Pot feet, which raise containers off the ground, can also help to prevent soggy compost, especially in winter when rainfall is heaviest. You can buy pot feet at the garden centre, but I make my own, cheaper versions using silicone cupcake moulds and quick-set premixed concrete. Simply mix the concrete with water and pour into the moulds. Then remove the moulds when they've set and pop these decorative feet under your pots.

Pretty protection

If you share a garden with squirrels, you will know that they love spring bulbs, turfing these tasty treats out of pots in autumn to eat or store for a snack later. This can be very disheartening when you have spent time and money planting them and anticipating a beautiful display the following year.

I have devised a few inexpensive barriers that keep squirrels at bay and look beautiful into the bargain. Collect some flexible thorny stems from roses or other prickly plants you have to hand, and cut them into different lengths. Then push them into the compost at each side of the pot to form a criss-cross pattern over the top, making sure they are secure, as squirrels will remove loose coverings.

To make a more robust cover to use year after year, wrap chicken wire around a large jar or cylindrical vessel a little smaller than the diameter of your pot. Trim it so there is an overlap and twist the wires on the cut edge to fix the seam together. Bring the chicken wire together at the top to make a cage and secure with garden twine, before plunging it into the compost to cover your potted bulbs.

Clockwise from top left: Make inexpensive pot feet to improve drainage from premixed concrete and silicon cupcake moulds; drill drainage holes into containers such as barrels with solid bases; use chicken wire pot covers or prickly stems cut from the garden to protect potted bulbs from squirrels.

Clockwise from top left: A simple pyramid for annual climbers such as sweet peas; this stem and twine support will keep tall perennials and annuals upright; twiggy stems pushed into the compost help to prevent spring bulbs flopping.

PROPS FOR FLOPPY BULBS

Spring bulbs such as hyacinths flop when their heavy flowerheads open, while the stems of paperwhite narcissi may also need some support. To keep these beauties upright, I prop them up with wooden chopsticks, which are given out for free with take-aways, or beech or hazel hedge trimmings. You can either tie individual stems to the sticks or natural supports with soft garden twine, or form a criss-cross barricade of sticks around the sides of the container to keep them in place.

SUPPORTING STRUCTURES

Pyramids and obelisks for climbers and supports for other plants with stems that tend to flop can be very expensive, but they are easy to make from natural materials in the garden, or other household items. Try these ideas to keep your plants on the straight and narrow.

Most climbers grown in pots will need a support for their twining stems or tendrils to wrap around, and making your own will not only save you a lot of money, but also allow you to create one to fit your pot perfectly.

The stems of other plants, including tall perennials such as asters, gaura, and border phlox, can flop, especially when grown in a windy site or where the light is restricted, causing them to lean towards the sun. To prevent the collapse of your plants, create simple supports to secure them.

Pyramids for climbers

These beautiful supports are ideal for growing annual sweet peas (*Lathyrus odoratus*), black-eyed Susans (*Thunbergia alata*), and the purple bell vine (*Rhodochiton atrosanguineus*), as well as compact clematis. To make them, you will need a few long, sturdy stems, pruned from a tree or large shrub such as hazel (*Corylus avellana*) or birch (*Betula*), or buy stems from coppicing companies (see p.186). You will also need some flexible growth from birch trees. If you don't have these stems, you can use some garden twine instead.

Perennial supports

Tall perennial plants can be supported with a structure that encircles the stems in your pot. They are best put in place in spring, so that the stems can grow through the latticework at the top and they will become almost invisible as the summer progresses.

To make them, cut a few sturdy stems about 60cm (24in) in length, or longer if you have very tall plants to support. First, plunge six or seven stems around the edge of the pot, burying them about 10cm (4in) deep in the compost. Then weave flexible stems or garden twine between these uprights around the sides. Attach separate lengths of twine to the top of the upright stems and string them across the top to create a latticework that the stems can grow through.

Wiring a wall

A cheap way to support larger climbers, such as jasmine, honeysuckle (*Lonicera*), and the cup and saucer vine (*Cobaea scandens*), is to fix inexpensive wires to a wall or fence, which these plants can then scramble along. Buy some vine eyes and a roll of heavy-duty galvanized wire from the garden centre. Screw one vine eye into the wall or fence on either side of the pot so that you can fix a length of taut wire horizontally between them. Repeat at 30cm (12in) intervals up the structure, to create a series of horizontal wires. Place the potted plant close to the wall and initially tie the stems to the wires with soft twine – they should then cling of their own accord.

CHAPTER 4
SPRING

Spring heralds the start of the growing season and, for me, it is a magical time of year, filled with hope and new life. I'm always excited to see the first of the bulbs in pots showing their faces by the front door and the rush that sowing seeds for my summer containers brings at this time of year, while enjoying the scents and colours of spring all around me.

PLANTS FOR SPRING

The joys of spring cannot be underestimated as the weather warms up and the bulbs I planted in autumn start to bloom, welcoming in the season with their colourful flowers. I'm always on the hunt for new plants to try at this special time, and for ways to propagate them, too.

To make the most of spring, you need to make preparations during the autumn, when inexpensive bulbs are planted (see p.131). If you wait until now, plants already in flower will cost three or four times as much, so it's well worth making a note in your diary in late summer to start planning the following year's display and buy or order some bulbs. The stars of the early spring show are daffodils, which you will find on pp.68–9, together with my other favourites, listed here.

Grape hyacinth (*Muscari*)
These gorgeous, undemanding spring bulbs flower reliably in their first year in pots of peat-free compost mixed with a handful or two of grit. You can then plant them in the ground where they will spread, allowing you to dig up clumps for your containers as they emerge in early spring in subsequent years. Choose from the common bright blue *Muscari armeniacum*, which self-seed readily in borders, or the larger-leaved *Muscari latifolium*, with

Grow a few grape hyacinths in small terracotta pots for a pop of spring colour.

Chives grow well in small pots of peat-free multi-purpose compost.

its eye-catching, duotone flowers. Other favourites are the pale blue 'Baby's Breath' and cool 'White Pearl' for contrast.

Allium (*Allium*)

There is an allium for every size of pot, from edible chives (*Allium schoenoprasum*) to *Allium hollandicum* 'Purple Sensation', with its tall stems topped with deep purple pompoms. Most flower in mid- or late spring, although one of my favourites, *Allium sphaerocephalon*, (see p.106) blooms later in the summer. Chives can be sown from seed, or buy young plants – I often buy a pot of them from the supermarket and divide the stems to make more plants (see p.25). Other alliums are available as bulbs in the autumn and flower the following year. The leaves of many plants develop first and wither as the flower stems emerge, so I tuck them behind other pots to disguise the dying foliage.

Wallflower (*Erysimum cheiri*)

These cottage garden favourites burst into bloom from early to mid-spring, when the knee-high stems produce sweetly scented flowers in an array of beautiful colours, from pastel shades to fiery oranges and reds. To save money, grow them from seed, sowing in late summer to flower the following spring. Or take cuttings of existing plants from mid- to late summer, which I find root very easily, cost almost nothing, and go on to create a great display the following year. Alternatively, buy bare-root plants in autumn.

Hyacinth (*Hyacinthus orientalis*)

The glamour girls of the bulb word, hyacinths are loved for their large heads of sweetly scented flowers, which will perfume the whole garden in mid-spring. Choose from the wide range of colours, including white, yellow, blue,

I grow my wallflowers from seed the previous summer to bloom in spring.

Place pots of hyacinths by the front door to greet visitors with their scent.

pink, red, and purple, and plant the bulbs in autumn, placing pots in a sheltered area and full sun. Prop up the heavy flower stems with twigs or chopsticks if they threaten to topple over. The bulbs keep from year to year if you allow the foliage to die down naturally and feed with a general purpose fertilizer after the blooms fade although I tend to plant them in the garden after the first year.

Primrose (*Primula*)
You can buy trays of colourful primroses and polyanthus, both species of *Primula*, in autumn and plant them in pots of their own or combine them with bulbs. They may flower a little over winter, but then really come into their own in spring. The plants are not particularly cheap, but you can keep these perennials from year to year. They prefer cool conditions in part shade, and I tip mine out of their pots and plant them in a border after they've flowered, where they thrive with no effort from me. I then pot them up again in autumn to add sparkle to my patio displays.

Chionodoxa (*Scilla forbesii*)
The tiny, starry flowers of this scilla appear just before the strappy foliage emerges. The blooms come in shades of blue, violet, or white and the plants are happy in sun or part shade. Plant the bulbs in pots of gritty compost in autumn. I've also planted some in the ground, which have spread and now offer free bulbs.

Crocus
The jewel-coloured flowers of these little bulbs appear very early in spring, and it is for this reason I grow a few in pots, although they are a bit like fireworks, going off with a bang but not lasting very long. Plant the bulbs in gritty

The dainty flowers of chionodoxa bloom for a few weeks in early spring.

Use trailing rosemary to cascade from a medium-sized container all year round.

compost in autumn, and mix them with other bulbs to create a longer display (see p.131).

Rosemary (*Salvia rosmarinus*)
One of my favourite herbs, drought-tolerant rosemary is easy to grow in a container, as it tolerates some neglect, even during the summer months. In spring, it produces small, blue flowers, which add to its charms. I also grow the trailing variety (*Salvia rosmarinus* Prostrata Group) in pots and hanging baskets, and take cuttings in summer.

Forget-me-not (*Myosotis sylvatica*)
No spring container display is complete without some forget-me-nots. These biennials produce leaves after germinating in their first summer, and then bloom the following spring, when they will add a frothy layer of tiny, sky-blue flowers to accompany your bulbs. Grow them from seed in early summer, to bloom the following year, after which they will self-seed.

Foam flower (*Tiarella*)
These ground-hugging perennials are among my favourites, and thrive in pots in sun or shade. Their deeply lobed, often bicoloured leaves overwinter and short spikes of tiny, star-shaped, white or pink flowers appear in spring. Remove the old leaves as new growth emerges in early spring.

Mossy saxifrage (*Saxifraga × arendsii*)
This ground-hugging saxifrage is easy to grow in pots and sports a mat of moss-like evergreen foliage and wiry stems, about 20cm (8in) tall, topped with tiny white, red, or pink flowers, which appear in late spring. I plant some in the border, where they spread and offer more plants to add to my pots in following years.

Perennial foam flowers are great value for money, blooming in pots year after year.

Crocuses are among the first flowers to show their heads in spring.

Clockwise from top left: These hoop petticoat daffodils (*Narcissus bulbocodium* 'Arctic Bells') add early spring colour; *Narcissus* 'White Lion' flowers from mid-spring; fragrant *Narcissus* 'Erlicheer' can be grown indoors or outside; *Narcissus poeticus*, with its scented white blooms with small, red-rimmed cups, is one of the last to flower.

Focus on daffodils

It's always exciting to see the first flower buds emerging between the strappy leaves of my daffodils (*Narcissus*), as we wave goodbye to winter and welcome in spring. These cheerful bulbs come in a range of colours, shapes, and sizes, from tiny dwarf types with little scented blooms, to flowers with large trumpets held on tall stems, and if you choose carefully, you can enjoy pots of these beauties from late winter to late spring.

For early blooms, try the hoop petticoat daffodils, which flower from late winter. The best for scent are the jonquils and Tazetta daffodils, such as *Narcissus* 'Sailboat' and 'Cheerfulness', and the tender paperwhites (see pp.160–1). For late spring flowers, I grow the elegant *Narcissus* 'Actaea', but there are hundreds to choose from, so take your pick.

Cut-price bulbs

While many daffodil bulbs are cheap to buy in the autumn, you will find that some cultivars are more expensive than others. If you have your heart set on a particular variety, club together with some friends and bulk buy from a wholesale nursery where prices per bulb will be lower, but there is usually a minimum order quantity. Waiting until later in autumn to buy bulbs can also save money, as retailers slash the prices to shift them. Your choices may be more limited then, but if the bulbs are firm and you plant them before Christmas, they should flower just as well as those planted earlier.

Growing daffs in pots

Plant daffodil bulbs in containers at two to three times their height (see p.131). Dwarf daffodils with smaller bulbs are ideal for window boxes, while the taller types will need a deeper pot. I do cheat sometimes, though, and plant the bigger bulbs in shallow pots, if that's all I have to hand, setting them in a sheltered spot to flower in the first year, and then removing them and planting them deeper in a bed or deeper pot of fresh compost to flower in subsequent years.

Plant the bulbs in peat-free compost mixed with a few handfuls of horticultural grit. Water well, then set your pots in a sunny or partly shaded area. Daffodil bulbs will flower without additional fertilizer in their first year, but water your pots during dry spells when they are in growth, until the foliage dies down, when they can tolerate drier conditions.

Aftercare

Daffodils bulbs are long-lived and will flower from year to year in a pot, given the right care. To keep them blooming, remove the faded flower heads promptly, and leave the foliage to die down naturally. This helps the plants restore their energy, ready to flower again the following spring.

When the new leaves emerge in spring, add a potassium-rich fertilizer every fortnight until flowering has finished and the leaves start to fade. I use my homemade comfrey feed (see pp.56–7) but you can buy plant-based organic fertilizer. If flowering deteriorates, try planting the bulbs in the ground, where they will have more access to moisture and nutrients.

Clockwise from top left: I buy cheap plug plants in spring; I then take cuttings from the plugs such as this *Leucanthemum* to create more; I have invested in a soil block maker, which compresses compost for seed sowing without a pot, saving money and reducing waste; repotting flagging plants in spring promotes new, healthy growth.

JOBS FOR SPRING

While the new growth and emerging bulbs are gifts for us to enjoy in spring, it's also the busiest time of year in the garden. However, I love this extra activity, which keeps my mind focused and helps me to relax.

While I am enjoying all the colourful bulbs popping up throughout spring, from tiny irises and crocuses to daffodils, hyacinths, and tulips, I remain mindful that I must start preparing for summer now to continue the show. I also look for self-sown plants to add to containers (see pp.32–3), and give potted shrubs and perennials their annual feed. Spring is also a good time to pot on any plants that have outgrown their homes.

Repot permanent plants

In early spring, I check my potted shrubs and perennials to see if any are flagging due to congested root growth, which will limit the plant's ability to take up water and nutrients. Tip smaller pots over and see if the roots are growing through the drainage holes, or, if you have a larger plant in a heavy container, push your finger into the top layer of compost to feel for compacted growth and check for roots growing on the surface.

To repot a root-bound plant, select a container one or two sizes larger than the original, and fill the base with a layer of peat-free potting compost. Water the plant well before removing it from its pot. If the roots are very congested and circling around the edges, use a sharp knife to gently score them, loosening the roots so they can grow into the new compost (do not worry if you cut some off, they will soon regrow). You can also tease them out with your fingers. Place the old pot on the layer of compost in the new container, and fill around it with more compost. Lift out the old pot and you will be left with a hole that fits the plant's root ball exactly. Pop the plant into the hole and firm around it, adding more compost if necessary and taking care not to bury the woody stems of shrubs or trees under the surface, which could rot them.

Sow seeds for summer pots

There are thousands of plants that you can grow from seed now to flower in your summer containers, but my favourites are perennials that bloom in their first year, including salvias, achilleas, dahlias, coneflowers (*Echinacea*), gaura (*Oenothera lindheimeri*), painted nettle (*Coleus*), and *Erigeron karvinskianus* (see pp.30–1). I sow other perennials that grow best in the ground long-term, such as delphiniums and lupins, in pots to flower in their first year before being transplanted into the garden.

I mix the perennials with long-flowering annuals, such as cosmos, zinnias, larkspur (*Consolida ajacis*), nasturtiums, sweet peas (see pp.134–5), *Salvia viridis*, morning glory (*Ipomoea tricolor*), marigolds (*Calendula*), heliotropes (*Heliotropium arborescens*), *Cerinthe major,* and pansies (see pp.146–7).

When buying seed, check whether it will grow into an annual, biennial, or perennial plant, so you know how long it will live, and if it is tender, half-hardy, or hardy, which will determine where the seeds need to be sown. For example, tender and half-hardy plants are sown indoors in spring, while hardy types will survive frosty periods outside. Then simply follow the instructions on pp.30–1.

Plant summer bulbs in pots

Buying dahlias, begonias, and lilies as plants can be very expensive, but you will find their tubers, corms, and bulbs are much more affordable. I plant mine in mid-spring, potting them up in containers of peat-free compost. Plant the sausage-like tubers of dahlias with the tip of the old flower stem sitting just below the surface. Begonias have small round corms, which you push gently into the top layer of compost in a tray or pot, with the hollow side facing up and exposed. Asiatic lilies are planted at a depth equal to the height of the bulb, with the pointed end facing upwards. Other lilies are planted at about two and a half times the height of the bulb.

Dahlias and begonias should be kept in a frost-free place until late spring when they can go outside; set pots of lilies in a sheltered sunny spot outside now.

Take dahlia cuttings

You can take softwood cuttings from the shoots that form from your dahlia tubers, increasing your plants for free. When the shoots are about 7.5cm (3in) long and have three sets of leaves, use a sharp knife to remove one at the base. Remove the bottom set of leaves from each cutting and pot them up in a 4:1 mix of peat-free potting compost and horticultural grit, with the remaining foliage exposed above the soil surface. Place them indoors in a warm, bright area, out of direct sun, and mist the compost to keep it damp.

Deadhead spring bulbs

To ensure your spring bulbs do not exert all their energy into making seed rather than bulking up the bulbs for next year's display, remove the flowerheads after they have faded. Another tip is to leave the foliage to die down naturally, since it acts like a rechargeable battery, feeding the plant and helping to guarantee next spring's flowers. Cutting off the leaves is like switching off the charger and your displays will suffer in subsequent years. Further boost the bulbs in spring by adding a high-potassium fertilizer, such as tomato feed, when the shoots appear, applying it every two weeks until the foliage starts to die back.

Buy young plants

If you only want one or two plants and have little space to sow trays of seeds, buy a few small, young plants in spring, which will be cheaper than mature specimens sold in larger pots later in the summer. Then simply move them into larger pots as they grow. Many garden centres sell perennials as young plants, known as plugs, in small paper pots now, which offer great value for money, especially since they will then go on to flower year after year. You can also propagate from these babies to make new plants for free (see pp.26–9).

Divide up and take cuttings

Making new plants from existing clumps by dividing them up (see pp.24–5) is a great way to increase your stock for container displays. Look for plants in borders or pots that could be divided to make new ones. I also take offsets in spring from succulents (see pp.112–3), such as houseleeks (*Sempervivum*) and *Echeveria*, as well as cuttings from shrubs such as hydrangeas, lavender, and herbs, rooting them in water (see p.29).

Clockwise from top left: Take dahlia cuttings now to make more plants for summer pots; deadhead bulbs such as daffodils after they have flowered; sow seeds for summer container displays, following the instructions on the seed packets.

MONEY-SAVING TIP

Remember that most seed packets come with a free tutorial on the back, so read it carefully for all the instructions you will need to grow that particular plant. You will find most of the advice you require, including times to sow, planting depths and aftercare.

SNAIL TRAILS

This simple method of rooting cuttings or sowing seeds is ideal if you don't have a lot of space for propagation indoors or outside. It saves money, too, since the materials you need are cheap and can be recycled, and it uses less compost than propagating in pots. Just follow these simple instructions to make your own snails.

Like many other gardeners I was wowed by this easy propagation method when I first saw it on social media, and now I would like to share my version of it with you. I make my snails from capillary matting, a strong, absorbent material that gardeners use to keep their greenhouse plants hydrated, which you can buy in rolls online or from the garden centre.

Here, I show you two methods: one for cuttings and the other for sowing seeds in a snail. Both are easy to do, and you will need the same tools and materials for each.

You will need
Recycled plastic, such as old compost bags
Capillary matting (optional)
Scissors
Peat-free seed and cuttings compost
Bowl
Cuttings or seeds
Twine
Multi-purpose compost
Pots for growing on cuttings and seedlings
Decorative pot

Snails for cuttings
1. Cut a strip of plastic about 45cm (18in) long and 15cm (6in) wide for cuttings. Cut a strip of capillary matting (which helps to retain more water, but is not essential) to the same size and soak it in a bowl of water.

Remove the matting, shake off excess water, and lay it over the plastic. Place the seed and cuttings compost in a bowl together with a little water to moisten it, then add a 2.5cm (1in) layer on top of the matting, as shown.

2. Lay your cuttings (see pp.26–9) on top of the compost, about 5cm (2in) apart and with the leaves over one edge, as shown.

3. Carefully roll up the snail from one end, taking care not to crush the delicate stems. Don't worry if some of the compost falls out as you do this.

4. Tie the snail together with three lengths of twine, as shown, securing them with a knot or bow. Place the snail on a tray and keep the cuttings in a frost-free area, out of direct sun. After a few weeks, roots will have developed on your cuttings, at which point you can unroll the snail (see overleaf). Then carefully remove the individual cuttings and transplant them into their own pots to grow on.

Watering your snail
Fill the tray with about 2.5cm (1in) of water and the matting and compost will draw up moisture from below, or water from above with a can. Check that the compost does not become too wet, which could rot the cuttings.

Snails for seeds

Follow Step 1 for snails for cuttings on p.75 to start making one for sowing seeds. You can cut the plastic and capillary strips a little narrower – about 10cm (4in) wide and 45cm (18in) long – for most seeds, or the same depth as for cuttings if growing deep-rooted plants such as sweet peas.

1. Roll up your snail and tie it with twine, as described in Step 2 on p.75. Stand your snail on a saucer or tray to stabilize it, and sow the seeds of your chosen plants carefully into the compost at the top. Sow evenly and at the depth recommended on the seed packet. I am using a stick here to make small holes to sow zinnia seeds at a depth of 0.5cm (¼in).

2. Place your snail in a frost-free place, if growing tender plants such as zinnias. Hardy types can go outside in a sheltered location with some protection from slugs and snails. I place mine on a table close to the house. Some seeds will germinate within a few days; others may take a couple of weeks. Continue to keep the snail moist as the seedlings grow (see Watering your snail on p.75). If you sowed tiny seeds and the seedlings are growing too close together, remove the weakest ones.

3. Once the seedlings have developed strong stems and a few sets of leaves, and you can see some roots growing at the bottom of the snail, unroll it to expose the individual rooted seedlings.

4. Carefully remove each seedling – they should lift out of the compost easily – and repot into larger containers of multi-purpose compost. I have reused plastic pots, which I had to hand, and planted five zinnias in each. These plastic pots then tuck neatly into my more decorative containers. Keep the plants watered for healthy, colourful flowers throughout the summer and early autumn.

MONEY-SAVING TIP

You can save even more money by reusing the capillary matting and plastic strips. After unrolling the snail and removing the seedlings or cuttings, simply rinse the materials in water and start again.

Holiday care for snails

A good tip if you are going away for a few days is to fill a tray with wet compost and place your snails on top. The roots at the bottom of the snails will then absorb the moisture in the compost and keep your seedlings and cuttings hydrated and healthy. This simple trick is a gamechanger and works really well.

CARING FOR CAMELLIAS

It's hard to resist the allure of camellias, their showy, colourful flowers lighting up the spring garden like fireworks against a backdrop of glossy, green leaves, providing a layer of colour above the bulbs. Here's how to grow them in pots and keep them blooming year after year.

Camellias are beautiful evergreen shrubs but they require acid soil to thrive, which means you may not be able to grow them in your borders. To find out, soil testing kits are available from garden centres, and if your soil is alkaline, you can simply grow them in pots.

To keep these shrubs happy, look for a large pot at least 25cm (10in) wide and deep, and buy peat-free ericaceous compost, which is acidic and offers the perfect home for them.

You will need
Large pot with drainage holes
Peat-free ericaceous compost
Camellia plant

1. Add a layer of ericaceous compost to the bottom of the pot. Water the camellia well, leave to drain, and then tip it out of its pot. Place the empty pot on the layer of compost.

2. Fill in around the empty pot with ericaceous compost, leaving a gap of about 5cm (2in) between the top of the compost and the rim of the pot.

3. Check the root ball of the camellia and loosen congested roots gently with a sharp knife or use your fingers. This will encourage them to grow into the compost and fill the container. Then remove the empty pot and slip the plant root ball into the hole.

4. Firm the compost around the plant to remove any large air pockets, and water well. Place in a cool, lightly shaded area to grow on and flower.

Aftercare

Each spring, apply a slow-release organic fertilizer formulated for acid-loving plants.

Camellias in pots prefer to be watered with rainwater from a butt, if possible. If you're using tap water, apply a tonic for acid-loving plants every week or two, following the application rates on the packaging, from spring to late summer. Products enriched with seaweed extracts offer a good balance of nutrients and minerals, and help to prevent the leaves from turning yellow.

You can reduce the plant's watering needs by adding a mulch of composted bark over the top of the compost.

Prune any wayward stems after flowering, if necessary, and repot it when the roots become congested, and you can see them growing at the top of the pot or through the drainage holes at the bottom.

Other acid-loving shrubs

Japanese maple (*Acer palmatum*); heather (*Calluna* and *Erica*); blueberries; *Pieris*; rhododendrons and azaleas (*Rhododendron*).

DIVIDING AURICULAS

I used to think of auriculas as old-fashioned until a friend bought me one and I fell in love with them. Their jewel-like blooms come in rich shades of purple, red, burgundy, and yellow, set off with contrasting eyes, and while plants can be expensive, they are easy to propagate.

Auriculas (*Primula auricula*) are related to European alpine primulas and became hugely popular in the 18th and 19th centuries, when these beauties were displayed on wooden shelves, known as auricula theatres. The little plants are popular again today, and you can display them in a theatre made from a pre-loved wooden shelving unit or just enjoy them as part of your patio display, and divide them to make more plants for free.

Auriculas are not completely winter-proof, disliking cold, wet weather, but they tolerate low temperatures, down to about -15°C (5°F), and will be happy in an unheated greenhouse, or under the eaves of a house, where they won't be drenched in rain.

You will need
Auricula plant
Clean, sharp knife
Small pots
Peat-free multi-purpose compost
Horticultural grit

1. Check your plant carefully in late spring or early summer after flowering for clusters of leafy stems that can be separated out. Using your hands, carefully prise apart sections with leaves and roots attached. If the roots are entwined and difficult to pull apart without damaging the plants, take a sharp knife and sever them, as shown. You may find that once you have separated the sections out, there are tiny shoots growing from the edges, which can also be removed to grow on.

2. Add a layer of 50:50 compost and grit to each pot, the plant the auricula divisions. Do not bury the leaves, which may rot if covered with damp compost. Fill in around the plant with the compost mix and firm gently.

3. Water the plants well, and stand them in a sunny area, protected from heavy rain, and leave to grow on.

4. Your auricula divisions may flower in the same year or following spring.

Aftercare
Water just enough to prevent the leaves from wilting. Feed with a high nitrogen fertilizer in early spring, followed by a weekly dose of potassium-rich fertilizer when in flower.

MONEY-SAVING TIP
If you don't own any auriculas, buy them after they've flowered, when they are often on sale and will be cheaper. New buys often comprise two or three plants, which can be divided, as shown here. If you only have one plant, move it to a larger pot to grow on and spread.

1.

2.

3.

4.

Clockwise from top left: This group of *Lomandra* 'White Sands', *Pittosporum tenuifolium* 'Silver Ball', and *Skimmia* x *confusa* 'Kew Green' will be happy on a sunny patio, balcony, or terrace year round if you water the plants regularly from spring to autumn.

LONG-LASTING SHRUB AND PERENNIAL MEDLEY

Hardy shrubs and perennials can save you both time and money, decorating containers with their flowers and foliage for many years, unlike expensive bedding plants that need to be replaced regularly. You don't need to compromise on looks, either, as this group proves.

One of the easiest ways to save money on your container displays is to include plants that will dress up your patio, terrace, or balcony for years to come. The investment you make initially may be higher than a pack of seasonal bedding plants that bloom for a few months, but divide that initial cost by four or five years, and you will see the annual savings they offer.

Some shrubs and perennials are available as cheaper bare-root specimens in winter (see also p.116), or you may find those that flower, such as the skimmia here, languishing in the "sale" section of your garden centre after they have bloomed, often at a substantial discount. I also take cuttings of shrubs in the garden to minimize the cost, and divide perennials in my borders to add to containers.

I've used an assortment of pre-owned and gifted pots to make this beautiful arrangement, which looks great all year but takes centre stage in winter and spring.

You will need
3 large pots
3 shrubs or perennials; those used here are:
  Skimmia × confusa 'Kew Green'; *Pittosporum tenuifolium* 'Silver Ball'; and the grass-like evergreen perennial *Lomandra* 'White Sands'
Peat-free soil-based compost
Peat-free ericaceous compost

1. Look for pots that will easily accommodate the root balls of each of your plants, with a little extra space for them to grow over the next few years.

2. Plant the *Pittosporum* and *Lomandra* as described on p.79 in peat-free soil-based compost, such as John Innes No. 3. This offers a good mix of nutrients and holds water better than multi-purpose. The skimmia prefers acidic conditions, so use peat-free ericaceous compost for this plant.

3. Leave a 2.5–5cm (1–2in) gap between the top of the compost and pot rim to allow space for watering. Firm the compost around the roots to remove any large air gaps.

4. Water the pots well and set them in a sunny or semi-shaded position. Spreading a bark chip mulch over the compost surface, leaving a gap around the stems, will help to lock in moisture for longer.

Aftercare
Water the plants well during dry periods and feed in spring with a balanced general purpose fertilizer. The skimmia needs a fertilizer for acid-loving plants (see Aftercare on p.79) and will prefer rainwater from a butt.

DIVIDING HOSTAS

Perfect for a cool, shady spot, hostas bring a lush, leafy note to patio displays. I use them as a counterpoint to colourful flowers and tuck them into corners where other plants struggle to thrive. They're easy to grow, too, and you can stretch your budget by dividing them up.

Hostas come in all shapes and sizes, from tiny dwarf types such as 'Blue Mouse Ears', with its mound of blue-green leaves, to large plants with foliage measuring up to 50cm (20in) such as 'Sum and Substance' and the giant blue hosta (*Hosta sieboldiana* var. *elegans*). Your choices are only limited by the size of your pots and the space you have to offer them.

Hostas like a dampish soil, so you will have to keep on top of watering those in containers. Their nemeses are slugs and snails, and while the larger, thicker-leaved varieties are more resilient to attacks, all can succumb by the end of the season. However, growing them in containers set on bricks in trays filled with water can help to protect them, while a grit mulch will offer extra slug control.

As a money-saving gardener, I like to get the best value from my hostas, and when tempted by a pretty plant at the garden centre, I look for one with lots of stems pushing through the compost that can be divided.

You will need
Hosta plant
Clean, sharp knife
Recycled plant pots
Peat-free multi-purpose compost
Decorative container with drainage holes in the bottom
Peat-free soil-based compost such as John Innes No. 3

1. The best time to purchase and divide hostas is in spring, when the leafy stems are just emerging. Check the height and spread of plants before buying to ensure you have space for them, and a pot to fit their root balls.

2. Water the plant well and then tip it out of its pot. Using a sharp, clean knife, make a small cut down the middle of the plant between the stems, then carefully prise apart the root ball with your hands. If the roots are too congested to do this, continue to cut them to form two clumps, each with leafy stems attached to some roots.

3. Plant one section in a reused plant pot filled with peat-free multi-purpose compost and pop the second clump back in its original pot with more compost to cover all the roots. Leave the plants in a cool spot outside.

4. When the divisions have put on some growth, transplant them into a container filled with peat-free soil-based compost.

Aftercare
Keep hostas watered from spring to autumn. Add a grit mulch to preserve moisture and deter slugs and snails. Feed every week or two from late spring to late summer with nitrogen-rich fertilizer – I use one made from stinging nettles (see pp.56–7).

1.

2.

3.

4.

CHAPTER 5
SUMMER

The most spectacular of all the seasons, summer is the time to enjoy the kaleidoscope of colours in your pots, while keeping plants well watered and fed, and removing fading flowers regularly to enjoy the longest displays. Taking a few cuttings here and there and sowing some seeds also helps me relax and keeps the show going as the months pass.

PLANTS FOR SUMMER

Summer's warm days and long evenings remind me of when I was a little girl, sitting on our balcony in Poland surrounded by pots and containers bursting with flowers of every shape, colour, and size. Here are my seasonal money-saving favourites to try in your containers.

You will find a huge choice of flowers and foliage plants for your pots at this time of year, and while it's easy to be lured by the array of bedding plants in bright, zingy colours, remember that most of these will last just one season and you may be shocked by the prices when you get to the till. To save money, I prefer to fill my summer pots with long-lived perennials and shrubs that flower year after year, and from which I can take cuttings. I also include annuals that I can sow from seed in spring for just a few pennies.

Coneflower (*Echinacea*)
These showy perennials produce shuttlecock-shaped flowers with a central orange cone surrounded by reflexed petals in colours ranging from white and pink to red and peach. The hip-height pink *Echinacea purpurea* is perhaps the easiest to grow from seed indoors in early spring, often flowering that same year, or try shorter varieties, such as *Echinacea purpurea* 'White Swan', orange 'Art's Pride' and 'Sombrero Salsa Red' – all ideal for smaller pots. Divide established plants in spring.

Echinacea 'Sombrero Salsa Red' is one of my favourites, producing vibrant blooms for pots.

Cosmos are easy to grow from seeds for summer-long colour.

Cosmos

Anyone who follows me on social media will know how much I adore these annual daisies, which are so easy to grow from seed in spring. With a wide range of colours to tempt you, and new varieties being launched almost every year, there's one for every size of pot. Sow the seed in trays or pots of peat-free seed compost indoors in spring and set the young plants outside when all risk of frost has passed.

Coleus (*Solenostemon scutellarioides*)

Loved for their decorative foliage, coleus make brilliant container plants for summer displays. They are available in a range of bright colours, with leaves ranging from red and pink to yellow and orange, as well as contrasting darker hues such as maroon and brown. Many have intricately patterned foliage and the serrated edges give rise to the plant's other common name, the painted nettle. In summer, these compact plants also produce spikes of small white or blue flowers. Coleus are tender perennials that are easy to grow from seed in spring, and you can overwinter them indoors. I also root a few stems in water in summer (see p.29) to grow more plants for free.

Pink (*Dianthus*)

Few plants can beat the sweet, clove-like scent of old-fashioned pinks, loved by my mother and grandmother. These sun-loving perennials are ideal for pots close to seating, and produce evergreen or semi-evergreen green-blue linear foliage, through which burst stems of small, fragrant flowers in summer. Among the best are the long-flowering pink and white 'Gran's Favourite', the cool white 'Memories', and the pale pink and red 'Doris'. Take cuttings in spring or summer.

Coleus are beautiful foliage plants, ideal for adding bright colours to a summer display.

I grow *Dianthus* 'Memories' for its spicy fragrance.

African lily (*Agapanthus*)

These South African perennials enjoy life in a pot, decorating a sunny patio or balcony with their spherical heads of white, blue, or purple flowers, held on tall stems above skirts of strappy foliage. They thrive in free-draining soil, so mix in some handfuls of grit with peat-free compost to create ideal conditions. I also feed mine regularly in summer with a high-potassium fertilizer to guarantee good results.

Gaura (*Oenothera lindheimeri*)

I wouldn't be without this wonderful money-saving plant, with its tall wands of starry white or pink flowers, which appear in succession for many months in summer. I grow this perennial in pots and in borders in full sun, sowing them from seed in early spring (they flower the same year). You can also take softwood cuttings from mature plants in early summer.

Dahlia

Few plants offer such a wide range of colours, shapes and sizes as dahlias, with too many to mention here. For small pots, choose compact varieties such as the Bishop series or go big and grow any you fancy. Grow dahlias in full sun, and feed them regularly in summer with a high-potassium fertilizer (see pp.56–7). In areas with cold winters, dig out the tubers after the first frost and store them indoors. However, on my sheltered patio they sail through the winter in pots beside the house. Take softwood cuttings (see p.26) in spring.

Fuchsia

You can buy hardy or tender fuchsias for pots, but for money-saving gardeners, I recommend the hardy types that overwinter and flower each year. These deciduous shrubs can grow up to a metre (3ft) or more in height, so check

Agapanthus flower from mid- to late summer and overwinter to bloom year after year.

Gaura is a perennial with tall wands of dainty flowers.

labels before buying for the size you want, as well as the flower colour and shape. All fuchsias cope with some shade. Root stems in water in spring or summer (see p.29).

Nemesia

A great choice for a window box or hanging basket, nemesias are compact, free-flowering perennials, often sold as annual bedding. They come in colours ranging from white and yellow through to pink and purple, and some are fragrant. While nemesias are not fully hardy, you may find they overwinter outside on a sheltered balcony or windowsill, or take cuttings and overwinter them indoors.

Purple top (*Verbena bonariensis* 'Lollipop')

This is a shorter form of the much-loved tall perennial species *Verbena bonariensis*, and produces the same little purple-domed flowers as the parent, but on 70cm (28in) stems, perfect for pots. Plants bloom all summer when grown in full sun, and will self-seed into cracks or gravel, but the seedlings will probably grow into taller plants, so bear that in mind. Alternatively, in summer, take softwood or semi-ripe cuttings that will come true to type.

Catnip (*Nepeta* × *faassenii* 'Kit Cat')

The mint-scented foliage of this perennial is loved by cats, hence the common name, but it is also loved by people for its small, lilac-blue flowers that appear from early summer to autumn. The compact 'Kit Cat' is perfect for pots and I've had mine for years in the same half barrel container. Clip it back after the first flush of flowers to encourage more to form. Perfect for pollinators, catnip is also easy to propagate from softwood cuttings, or try growing it from seed in spring.

I grow a few dahlias in pots on the patio, where I can see the detail in their exquisite flowers.

Nepeta × *faassenii* 'Kit Cat' attracts a host of pollinators.

Focus on lavender

As many of you may know, I have grown a whole hedge of lavender in my garden from cuttings and it's a plant I never tire of, offering evergreen scented foliage and spikes of mauve, purple, or white fragrant flowers, loved by pollinators, in summer.

There are many different types to choose from, including French lavender (*Lavandula stoechas* subsp. *stoechas*), English lavender (*Lavandula angustifolia*), lavandin (*Lavandula × intermedia*) – a long-flowering hybrid of English lavender and *Lavandula latifolia* – as well as many different cultivars.

Choosing lavenders

I've grown a few lavenders on my patio over the years and the best I've found for medium-sized pots are the highly scented English types, *Lavandula angustifolia* 'Hidcote' or 'Munstead'. For larger containers, try the tall *Lavandula × intermedia* 'Phenomenal' or 'Grosso', and the white 'Edelweiss'.

While most lavenders do well in pots, I've never managed to overwinter a French variety. They're not very hardy and are more sensitive to over- or underwatering, so to save money, I would opt for one of the other types.

How to grow lavender in pots

When growing lavender in pots always use a gritty mix and ensure the pot or container has drainage holes in the base. Place plants in full sun, with plenty of air circulation around their stems – for this reason, I always advise growing them in pots of their own.

Before you start planting, combine a 4:1 mix of peat-free multi-purpose compost and grit in a large bucket, then add a few handfuls of sand to create free-draining conditions for your plant. Add a layer to the base of a suitable pot, and plant the lavender as for a shrub (see pp.78–9), firming around the roots to remove large air gaps. Also leave a space of 5cm (2in) between the surface of the compost mix and the rim of the pot, to allow space for watering.

Apply a 2.5cm (1in) gravel mulch on top of the compost, which will help to maintain the right level of moisture around the roots, while preventing soil splashing up on to the leaves. It also gives the pot a lovely decorative finish. Place the pot on feet (see pp.58–9) so that water can drain easily out of the holes at the bottom. Water and place in full sun in a sheltered spot, out of cold wind and where it will be protected from heavy rain in winter.

Aftercare

Water the lavender about once a week from spring to autumn – guard against overwatering which may lead to root rot. Do not water in winter, when the plant is dormant.

Lavenders generally do not need feeding, but English lavender and lavandin benefit from pruning after flowering in late summer or in early spring, to prevent them becoming woody and to extend their lifespan. Cut the stems down to a live, green shoot, as the plants won't regenerate from old, brown stems. If you want to give French lavender a go, deadhead it regularly, otherwise it will stop flowering.

Lavender is a relatively short-lived shrub so do not be disappointed if after a few years it starts underperforming. At this point, take semi-ripe cuttings in summer (see p.26) to grow more plants and replace those that are looking leggy and failing to flower well.

Clockwise from top left: *Lavandula* 'Ballerina' is a beautiful French lavender with purple and white flowers; this compact lavender was grown from a seed from one of my English types; *Lavandula angustifolia* 'Hidcote', ideal for smaller pots; *Lavandula × intermedia* 'Grosso' is a large plant, best grown in big tub or half barrel.

Focus on salvias

As the sun rises higher in the sky, my salvias start to twinkle in their pots, ushering in the long, lazy days of summer. A gift for money-saving gardeners, the perennials and shrubs are easy to propagate from cuttings taken in late spring or summer, which provide a lifeline for the more tender types that may suffer during a cold, wet winter. The annuals are also easy to grow from seed in spring. All salvias enjoy free-draining growing conditions and will flower best in full sun.

Choosing salvias for pots

There are many decorative salvias that enjoy life in pots of gritty compost, as well as the herb sage (*Salvia officinalis*), which will be happy growing for many years in a large pot or half barrel.

My favourites include Balkan clary (*Salvia nemorosa*), a hardy perennial, with aromatic grey-green foliage and knee-high spikes of violet-purple flowers. The cultivar *Salvia nemorosa* 'Caradonna' is particularly beautiful, with vibrant flowers on purple-black stems. Another perennial that always makes me smile is *Salvia* 'Amistad', with its tall, dark stems of bright purple trumpets, ideal for the back of a patio display. This variety is not very hardy, but cuttings take easily in water and can be overwintered on a windowsill indoors until the following year. *Salvia patens* is smaller than 'Amistad' but with similar shaped sky-blue flowers in summer. It, too, is not fully hardy but stems root easily in a glass of water.

Left *Salvia* 'Amistad' is one of my favourites, its tall spikes of rich purple tubular flowers blooming from midsummer until the frosts.

The shrubby *Salvia* × *jamensis* and its many cultivars is also hardy and produces a mound of evergreen leaves threaded with slim stems of small flowers with lip-like petals. You may have seen the popular white and red 'Hot Lips'; others include the dark plum 'Nachtvlinder' and bright pink 'Raspberry Royale'. All do well in pots and flower for many weeks in summer.

I also love the annual *Salvia viridis* 'Blue Monday', which is easy to grow from seed and makes a wonderful cut flower.

Planting up

Most salvias prefer a free-draining 50:50 mix of peat-free soil-based compost such as John Innes No. 1 and horticultural grit. If you have moles, try adding a layer of the soil from their hills to the base of the pot, which offers prefect conditions for these plants. Do not bury the stems beneath the compost and leave a 2.5–5cm (1–2in) gap between the surface and pot rim for watering.

Aftercare

Although salvias are drought-tolerant, you will need to water those in pots about twice a week from spring to early autumn. However, only irrigate when the compost surface feels dry. Salvias are more likely to sail through a cold winter if their compost is dry, so protect plants from heavy rain to get them through.

Feed plants from spring to late summer with a high-potassium fertilizer (see pp.56–7) and deadhead regularly to prolong flowering until the first frosts. Support tall salvia varieties with twiggy prunings from the garden.

JOBS FOR SUMMER

Summer is a time of plenty, and my patio is brimming with flowers, herbs, and easy crops in pots, which are fun to add into the mix. Of course, containers need watering throughout the summer months, but water can be expensive, so use it wisely by following the tips below.

While most of the sowing and bulb planting is completed and we can relax a little by the time summer rolls around, if you want a long-lasting, flower-filled container display that lasts all season, it's important to keep on top of feeding and watering, and removing faded blooms regularly.

Watering and mulching

Container plants can soon become parched during the warmer months, so make sure you add a mulch over the surface of the compost (see pp.54–5) and direct your watering can over the root area, rather than splashing it on the flowers and foliage. Give your pots a long drink each time you water, and remember that rain may not top up a container if a plant's foliage is covering the rim and it just pours over the sides, so water if the compost feels dry, whatever the weather.

A water butt is a great investment (see p.54), but if you don't have space for one, use waste water from the kitchen to save money on bills. I always wash my fruit and vegetables over a bowl and tip the water on my containers outside. If you have a fish tank, you can use the dirty water when you're cleaning it out, too – all the residue from the fish is packed with nutrients that will feed your plants!

Water either early in the morning when it's cooler, or better still, in the evening, since water does not evaporate much at night.

Set tender plants outside

If you sowed the seeds of tender or half-hardy plants in spring, the seedlings can be planted outside in their final pots in the first weeks of summer, after the frosts. Tender bulbs such as dahlias and begonias are also ready to plant outside at this time, together with young plants and cuttings that have been growing indoors. Pack plants into their pots at closer distances than those recommended on the seed packets for a bountiful display.

I've included a range of themed displays in this chapter to inspire you, but I would also encourage you to experiment, since you have little to lose when your plants cost just a few pence to grow. I've created many beautiful containers by throwing caution to the wind.

Deadheading

You can often prolong your pot displays if you remove the faded heads from the flowers, known as deadheading, every few days. I find this job very therapeutic, as it not only prompts many annuals and some perennials to continue to make new flowers, extending their performance, but also keeps my potted plants looking neat and tidy.

Cutting a few stems from your pots for indoor vases has the same effect, promoting new flowering stems, while also allowing you to make some posies for the house or to give as sustainable gifts (see project on pp.102–3).

Clockwise from top left: When deadheading, take the flowering stem back to the base of the plant, or to the leaf below the flower; feed fruit plants and flowers with a potassium-rich feed now; after blooming, cut back lavender to green shoots lower down on the flowering stems, to prevent plants becoming woody; dunk very dry potted plants in a tray of water to rehydrate them.

Take cuttings of shrubs such as lavender in summer and set them outside in a sheltered spot, but remember to water them regularly. The warmth and moisture will soon prompt new root growth.

Feeding

Start feeding your plants about six weeks after planting them in fresh potting compost, when the fertilizer it contains will have been used up. One way to remember to feed and guard against giving plants too much is to select a day of the week to fertilize. I came up with Feeding Friday, which reminds me to do it each week.

For leafy growth, I use nitrogen-rich fertilizer, and then, as soon as buds appear on flowering and fruiting plants, such as peonies, agapanthus, and Mexican fleabane (*Erigeron karvinskianus*), I add a potassium-rich feed. I make them myself from nettles and comfrey (see also pp.56–7) but if you don't have access to these plants, buy plant-based organic fertilizers from the garden centre.

Propagate now for autumn pots

I love living in the moment, but I'm always thinking ahead, too, so that I will have more plants to boost my wellbeing as the seasons turn. Sowing autumn bedding plants such as violas, pansies, and *Bellis perennis* in pots of seed compost in early summer is a lovely pastime and the seedlings can grow on outside, with some protection from slugs and snails. Primulas can be divided now, too, to make new plants for autumn pots (see pp.24–5).

Disarming pests

No one wants to see their prized plants nibbled down to stubs by slugs and snails, and while not all molluscs are plant-eaters, many sadly are. I set pots of vulnerable plants on bricks in trays of water and add grit over the compost to deter them. Or place plants on tables or chairs that are not as easy for slugs and snails to access, and remove any hiding behind your pots during the day.

PRE-HOLIDAY SNIP

I cut off all the flowers from my container plants just before I go away on holiday, prompting them to make new blooms. I come home to a beautiful floral display as by then the plants will have developed new flowers.

Holiday container care

I love the holiday season when I can relax with my boys, but I always worry that my container plants may suffer while I am away, so I have come up with a way of helping them to survive this period of neglect. If you're going away for a week or two, group your pots in a cool, shady area where evaporation rates will be lower, and place them in shallow trays filled with water. These will store enough water to keep them hydrated while you're away, as the compost draws up moisture through the pots' drainage holes in the bottom.

Plants for free

Many plants root easily from cuttings taken in summer. Take softwood cuttings early in the season from shrubs such as fuchsia, *Viburnum*, and lavender, and perennials, including salvias, gaura, catmint (*Nepeta*), pelargoniums, and herbs. Later in summer, as the stems mature, take semi-ripe cuttings (see p.26) from plants that are frost tender and won't survive winter, such as *Salvia* 'Amistad' and pelargoniums. I also prune my potted rosemary after flowering in early summer, and pop the cut stems in water to root and make new plants for free.

CUT FLOWER CONTAINER

Cut flowers are wildly expensive and many have travelled halfway across the world to decorate our homes, so to save both money and the planet I like to grow a few of my own, which is very easy if you have a large, pre-loved container such as this old chest.

This is a very simple project for anyone with sunny space for a large container to house a few beautiful cut flower plants. I grew some from seed in the spring, took cuttings from an existing plant and grew them on for the perennial *Verbena* and treated myself to a few new plants, from which I will save seed or take cuttings later in the season to create free plants for my pots next year. Also look out for young perennial plug plants earlier in spring (see p.70 and p.72) to save money.

Once planted and established, you can cut a few stems every week to decorate your home. The plants will soon recover and develop more flowering stems to pick a few weeks later.

You will need
Large pre-loved container
Old compost bag (for lining if needed)
Peat-free multi-purpose compost
Selection of plants. Those used here are:
Ageratum houstonianum 'Blue Planet';
Florist's dill (*Anethum graveolens* 'Mariska');
Baby's breath (*Gypsophila paniculata*);
Nicotiana 'Tinkerbell'; annual clary (*Salvia viridis* 'Blue Monday'); *Verbena rigida* 'Santos Purple'

1. To save my chest from rotting quickly when exposed to wet compost, I lined it with old compost bags. Ensure both the container and bags have drainage holes in the base. I have filled the base with the soil from mole hills to save money on compost, but if you don't have these, try a layer of old, upturned plant pots or used compost. Then top up your container with new multi-purpose compost.

2. Set out your plants, still in their pots, to create an arrangement you are happy with, checking that tall plants won't shade the shorter ones, as they are all sun-lovers.

3. Water the plants, then plant them at the same level they were sitting at in their pots, firming the compost gently around the roots.

4. Make sure you leave a gap of about 5cm (2in) between the rim of the container and the compost for watering, then give the plants a good soak.

Aftercare
Water the container regularly and feed weekly with a potassium-rich fertilizer from now until the beginning of autumn. The hardy plants will then overwinter, but take cuttings of the tender *Ageratum* and clary.

Other plants to try
Achillea; cloud grass (*Agrostis nebulosa*); *Ammi majus*; *Cerinthe*; cosmos; strawflowers (*Helichrysum bracteatum*); statice (*Limonium*); *Phacelia tanacetifolia*; zinnias.

1.

2.

3.

4.

1.

2.

3.

4.

PROPAGATED HYDRANGEAS

Elegant flowers and decorative seedheads make hydrangeas one of my favourite plants and I always have a few growing in pots on the patio, but they can be expensive, so I propagate mine to make more for free.

Hydrangeas come in a huge range of colours, from red and pink to purple, blue and white, and they perform really well in large pots, flowering from year to year with just a little annual care and regular watering from spring to early autumn. However, I'm always taken aback by the price of these shrubs at the garden centre and online, so to save money, I propagate them from the plants I already have growing in the garden and in pots to make more for free.

You will need
Hydrangea plant
Spade (if digging out plant from a border)
Clean, sharp secateurs
Large used pot
Peat-free multi-purpose compost or ericaceous compost for blue varieties

1. In early spring, check your hydrangea for new growth emerging beneath the old flower heads, and cut back each of the stems to a healthy new bud. Water the plant well and tip it out of its pot, or dig it up from the garden, if it's not too large. Alternatively, dig a trench around bigger border plants to expose the roots.

2. Check for shoots growing around the edge of the root ball, away from the mother plant in the centre. Using sharp secateurs, carefully cut out a shoot with some roots attached to it.

3. Continue around the plant, carefully removing more baby plants. One large plant may offer up to four or five shoots.

4. Fill a large pot with peat-free multi-purpose or soil-based compost, or ericaceous compost if your hydrangea has blue flowers (the blooms are likely to turn pink if you plant it in ordinary compost). Plant the stems in the compost at the same level they were growing at in their original pot or in the ground. Leave a gap of about 5cm (2in) between the top of the compost and rim of the container for water to collect. Firm the compost around the roots and water well.

Aftercare
Water the new shoots regularly from spring to early autumn. They will put on new growth as the season progresses but may not flower until the following year, although I've found that some, such as *Hydrangea arborescens* 'Annabelle', often bloom later in the summer.

These shrubs are deciduous and will lose their leaves over winter. When you see new growth emerging in spring, prune the stems as described in Step 1 above, and apply a nitrogen-rich fertilizer every week or two, until they start to produce buds. I then switch to a potassium-rich feed (see pp.56–7), which will encourage the plant to develop lots of beautiful flowerheads during the summer and early autumn.

FLORAL SYMPHONY

To create a sparkling eye-catcher on your patio, think big and use large containers such as a half barrel packed with a combination of long-flowering shrubs, bulbs, and perennials that perform all summer.

The trick to creating a long-performing summer display is to pack different types of plants into a large container, and to save money include those that will overwinter and flower again from year to year.

For this arrangement, I've used a silverbush (*Convolvulus cneorum*) that holds the display together with its silvery evergreen foliage and pink-budded white summer flowers. The pink and white *Salvia* 'Amethyst Lips' provides pops of colour. This bushy shrub blooms all summer and should overwinter in all but the coldest gardens – take cuttings in late summer (see p.26) as an insurance policy if you live in a cold region. The gaura (*Oenothera lindheimeri* 'Whirling Butterflies') is one of my favourite perennials because it's very easy to grow from seed and cuttings and adds height and dainty white summer blooms throughout the summer. The hardy *Allium sphaerocephalon*, with its little egg-shaped, dark red blooms, is easy to grow from inexpensive bulbs planted in pots in the autumn. It will also appear year after year from an initial planting.

I like to add a few trailing plants to spill gracefully over the sides of the container. Here, I've used the tender annual silver nickel vine (*Dichondra argentea* 'Silver Falls'), with its sparkling foliage, which I grew from seed in spring. I've also included the trailing white flowers of bacopa (*Chaenostoma cordatum* 'Snowflake'), which you can sow from seed each spring, or take cuttings to overwinter it.

You will need
A range of small shrubs, perennial flowers, and bulbs, such as those listed on the left
Large container with drainage holes
Peat-free multi-purpose or soil-based compost

1. Set the container where it will be sheltered from heavy rain in winter. Then fill with peat-free compost (see also p.102 for tips on saving money on compost), leaving a gap of about 5cm (2in) between surface and the rim.

2. Add the taller plants such as the gaura and silverbush in the centre or to one side. Be mindful of where the sun faces, and ensure they won't overshadow the shorter plants.

3. Plant the trailing bacopa and silver nickel vine around the sides. These are quite vigorous plants so leave gaps between them and they will soon grow to fill the spaces.

4. Finally, squeeze the alliums into any gaps between the other plants. Water well and wait for the show to begin.

Aftercare
Water the plants regularly and feed weekly in summer with a high-potassium fertilizer (see pp.56–7). Clip the silverbush after it's flowered to prompt a second flush of blooms, and deadhead the gaura regularly.

The main plants in this beautiful container display will bloom year after year on a sheltered patio, while the tender annual trailing plants can be sown from inexpensive seed each spring. For early season interest you could plant some little spring bulbs such as crocuses and dwarf daffodils in the autumn.

1.

2.

3.

4.

A ROSE GARDEN IN POTS

Roses are so meaningful and I have many that have been gifted to me by friends and family that I cherish. While most are in my borders, I keep a few in pots on the patio, where I can enjoy the flowers up close.

I love roses but they are very expensive to buy, so for my containers, I simply take cuttings from those I have growing in the garden. This has many advantages, not only because the new plants that grow from them are free, but also because I know exactly what size, colour, and scent I will be getting and can choose compact varieties that are suited to containers.

The easiest way to make new roses is to take hardwood cuttings from late autumn to late winter, after the leaves have fallen (see pp.26–9). This method is one of the easiest forms of propagation, and you can keep them in the garden or in a pot. Water them frequently from spring to early autumn to prevent the roots drying out. Hardwood cuttings require patience and you may have to wait up to a year before potting them up, as shown here, but in many cases they may then flower the following year.

You will need
Rose cuttings
Peat-free multi-purpose compost
Recycled plant pots
Large container
Peat-free soil-based compost
 such as John Innes No. 3

1. Leave your cuttings for about a year, and by late autumn or early winter, the stems should have formed healthy new roots and a few sets of new leaves.

2. Then, dig the cuttings out of the ground, or tip them out of their pot.

3. Select recycled pots that will accommodate the new roots and some extra growth and plant each cutting in its own container filled with peat-free compost. Do not bury the stems under the surface, which may rot them.

4. Set the young roses on a sunny patio, watering during dry spells. In spring or early summer, transplant them into their final pots. Choose a deep container with plenty of space for growth, and plant in soil-based compost (see also pp.78–9 for planting technique). Water well and prune the stem tips lightly to promote bushier growth.

Aftercare
Keep your roses well watered during dry spells and feed them every one to two weeks during the spring and summer with a potassium-rich fertilizer (see pp.56–7).

PLANT BREEDERS RIGHTS
Buying a strong rose variety suitable for pots from a reputable specialist is a good investment, but remember that most roses are protected by Plant Breeders Rights, which means you can only take cuttings for your own use in a private garden.

COLOURFUL COLANDER

As a money-saving gardener, I'm always looking for planting ideas that don't cost a fortune to decorate my patio in summer, and this beautiful display of succulents housed in an old colander fits the bill perfectly.

Many hanging baskets dry out very quickly and are difficult to maintain, but this group of succulents in their preloved container are drought-tolerant and will sail on through summer unscathed. The colander, which I found in a second-hand shop, comes complete with drainage holes, and the plants have all been grown from cuttings which I took about a year ago and potted up in the autumn, but you can, of course, buy new plants too.

To make plants for free, take offsets from sedums, houseleeks (*Sempervivum*), and other succulents in autumn. Detach the baby plants (offsets) growing around the edge of mother plant by either pulling them away with your fingers or using a sharp knife to sever them. Ideally, the offsets should have a few roots attached to the leaves, but I have found that many seem to grow even without roots. Plant in a 50:50 mix of peat-free multi-purpose compost and grit, gently pushing those with no roots into the top layer of compost.

You will need
An old colander
Piece of plastic for lining (I used an old potting compost bag)
A range of succulents. Those used here are: *Sempervivum* 'Noir'; *Sedum tetractinum* 'Coral Reef' and *Sedum kimnachii*
4:1 mix of peat-free multi-purpose compost and horticultural grit
Chopstick

1. Line the colander with a sheet of reused plastic, making a few holes in the base for drainage. The plastic helps to insulate the plants from the hot metal and retains more moisture than the colander.

2. Fill the colander with the gritty compost mix and plant the largest succulent (I've used a *Sempervivum* 'Noir') in the centre.

3. Using a chopstick, carefully remove the smaller succulents from their trays (if using offsets) and plant them around the sides, creating a mosaic of different colours and textures. Firm in gently with your fingers.

4. Make sure you leave a gap between the top of the compost and the rim of the colander to allow water to accumulate. Then water well, avoiding the leaves if possible, and place in a sheltered, sunny position outside.

Aftercare
Water the container when the top of compost feels dry – guard against overwatering, which these drought-lovers will resent – and do not feed them, since they are adapted to growing in poor soil conditions. Not all the plants here are fully hardy, so the colander display may need to spend the winter indoors in cold areas – I left it outside by the house, but you could use it to decorate a sunny windowsill inside.

STYLISH SUCCULENTS

Succulents such as the houseleek tree make a dramatic statement in a pot or basket and are easily propagated. I've edged this display with a frilly necklace vine, also propagated from cuttings.

The rosettes of red fleshy leaves that adorn the houseleek tree (*Aeonium arboreum*) are both intriguing and beautiful, and while these plants can grow up to 1.2m (4ft) or more in their native Iberian homeland, when grown in a pot they will generally reach about half that height. To save money, buy one plant and use it to propagate others, following the tips below. While the houseleek tree is not hardy, it's a dual-purpose plant, creating a decorative container display outside in summer and a pretty houseplant in the winter.

The necklace vine (*Muehlenbeckia complexa*) softens the edge of the pot, and although it's not completely hardy either, it survives the winter on my sheltered patio in a pot tucked up close to the house wall. I also propagate it in late summer in water (see p.29) for back-up, in case I lose those outside in winter.

You will need
Aeonium arboreum plant
Glass of water
Small pots
Peat-free cuttings compost
Horticultural grit
Decorative planter with drainage holes
Peat-free multi-purpose compost
4 small *Muehlenbeckia complexa* plants

1. Cut a rosette from your *Aeonium* plant with 10–15cm (4–6in) of stem. Pop it in 2.5cm (1in) of water in a glass so the stem base is submerged but the rosette is kept dry. Repeat with a few more rosettes. Set in a bright spot.

2. Change the water every few days to prevent it becoming stagnant. When roots form, fill small pots with a 4:1 mix of cuttings compost and horticultural grit. Make holes, then plunge the rooted stems into the gritty mix. Keep the cuttings just moist, watering when the compost feels dry.

3. Leave the cuttings to grow on. If you start in summer, they should have grown into sizeable plants by the following summer. Then fill a decorative pot with a 50:50 mix of peat-free multi-purpose compost and grit, and plant up your young *Aeonium* plants.

4. Add the *Muehlenbeckia complexa* around the edge of the pot and set in full sun.

Aftercare
Only water when the top of the compost feels dry. In autumn, before the frosts arrive, bring the pot indoors to decorate your home.

PRUNE FOR MORE ROSETTES
As your cuttings mature, remove the rosettes growing at the tip of each stem to encourage bushier growth with more rosettes. The rosette you removed can also be used as a cutting.

MONEY-SAVING PEONIES

Many perennials such as peonies can be bought in winter as bare-root plants, which are much cheaper than potted pots sold later in the year. Check online for these deals and pot up your peonies when they arrive.

Bare-root plants are available for a limited time from late autumn to early spring, and if you can wait until the end of the season, when nurseries keen to shift their stocks often offer them at even greater discounts, you can save even more money.

When the rootstocks arrive, they will look very unpromising, and may remain dormant until early spring, at which time you will notice shoots beginning to develop. A few weeks later, the plant will be unrecognizable and look like those on sale at the garden centre for almost double the price!

Choose compact herbaceous peonies for your patio pots, rather than tree peonies, which are shrubs and grow into large plants. Flower colours include white, yellow, red, and pink, and many have a spicy scent and plants bloom in early summer. The pretty foliage is another bonus and continues to offer interest after the flowers fade. I grow my peonies in old plastic pots and bring them on to the patio when they are about to bloom, placing them in ornamental pots. After they've flowered I keep them in situ for their foliage, then move them to a quiet spot as the leaves die down.

You will need
Bare-root peony (*Paeonia*)
Recycled pot
Peat-free multi-purpose compost
Decorative pot with drainage holes
Peat-free soil-based compost

1. Unwrap your bare-root plants as soon as they arrive and soak the roots in a bowl of water for about 30 minutes.

2. Meanwhile, select a recycled plant pot that will accommodate the root ball and add a layer of peat-free multi-purpose compost to the base. Place the peony's roots on top and fill in around them with more compost, making sure any shoots are above the surface.

3. Water well, and store in a sunny spot to grow on. After a few weeks, new leafy stems will appear, and you can then plant them in their final pot.

4. Choose a deep container, and plant in peat-free soil-based compost such as John Innes No. 3, leaving a gap of about 5cm (2in) between the surface and pot rim for watering. Place the potted plants in a sunny area.

Aftercare
Water your peony during the growing season and feed from early spring until early summer with a potassium-rich fertilizer (see pp.56–7). Cut back dead stems in autumn. Once your peonies are well established, you can divide them in the autumn (see pp.24–5).

Other bare-root plants to try
Agapanthus; *Astrantia*; hostas; hardy geraniums; *Heuchera*; *Nepeta*; salvias.

Money-saving peonies in containers bring my patio to life in spring with their big, colourful blooms and lush, divided leaves, which create a textured backdrop for other plants after the flowers fade.

1.
2.
3.
4.

CLIMBING CUCAMELONS

If you're looking for an edible snack to grow on your patio that looks as good as it tastes, try cucamelons. These little mini melons actually taste of cucumber and lime, and they're cheap and easy to grow.

I tried growing cucamelons (*Melothria scabra*) for the first time this year after a friend recommended them and I'm so pleased with the results. The plant is a tender vine native to Central and South America and produces trailing or climbing stems that deliver high yields of pretty, grape-sized fruits in summer.

I made a support for the vines from stems from my garden, or use four of five bamboo canes tied at the top with strong garden twine.

You will need
Cucamelon seed (*Melothria scabra*)
Peat-free seed compost
Reused small pots or seed trays
Large decorative pot with drainage holes
Peat-free multi-purpose compost
Home-made plant support (see pp.60–1)

1. Sow your cucamelon seeds indoors in spring in pots or trays of peat-free seed compost at a depth of 1cm (½in) with the blunt end facing downwards. Keep in a warm area and the seeds should germinate within a couple of weeks. When the seedlings are large enough to handle, transfer them to small pots of their own to grow on indoors.

2. After the frosts in late spring or early summer, push an obelisk into a large pot of peat-free multi-purpose compost. Plant the cucamelons next to the support, and firm in gently to remove any large air gaps.

Four cucamelons plants will be fine for a large pot such as the one I've used here. Tie the plants to the support with soft twine until they cling of their own accord.

3. Once the main shoot of each cucamelon has reached about 2m (6ft), pinch out the growing tip at the top and pinch out the side shoots when they are 40cm (16in) in length.

4. Keep watering your pot of cucamelons regularly, and harvest the fruits from midsummer to early autumn when they are the size of grapes.

Aftercare
Feed your cucamelons once a week during the growing season with a high potassium feed. When ready, harvest the cucamelons every few days, which will encourage more to form.

MONEY-SAVING TIP
Most people grow cucamelons from seed each year, but the plants also produce tubers that can be kept over the winter indoors. At the end of the season, cut down the plants and dig out the little tubers, then store them in pots of just-moist compost in a frost-free place. Plant up in pots of cuttings compost in spring, then set outside again after the frosts.

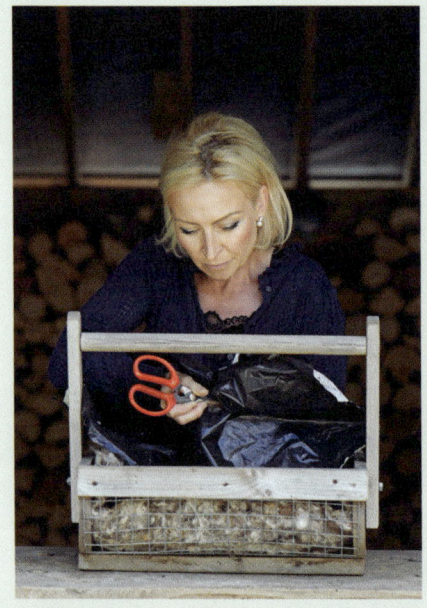

1.

2.

3.

NEW FRUIT PLANTS FOR FREE
Summer-fruiting strawberries produce long stems with baby plants at the end (runners), which you can pot up in late summer to make new plants (everbearers don't produce many runners). Place your basket where you can plant the runner, still attached to the parent plant, in a pot of peat-free multi-purpose compost. Peg down the stem with a U-shaped piece of wire to keep the plantlet in place. Keep the runner watered and sever the stem from the parent plant when the baby has established a good root ball.

STRAWBERRY SURPRISE

The delicious, sweet taste of strawberries is synonymous with summer days, and despite their high cost in the shops, they're among the cheapest and easiest fruits to grow on a patio, balcony, or window box.

We grow most of our edibles in our veg patch in the garden, but I always like to include a few strawberry plants in pots on the patio, where the fruits are easy to pick as they ripen. The most cost-effective way to grow them is to order "runners" from reputable suppliers from late summer to early autumn. Another way to source plants is to join a gardening society or group, where people often share runners for free.

Choose from early-, mid-, and late-fruiting summer cultivars, or perpetual strawberries, or everbearers as they're also known, which produce flushes of smaller fruits from early summer to autumn. If you have space, you could try a few of each type for a long season of fruit.

You will need
Large, deep basket
Wool from online packaging
Compost bag for lining
Peat-free multi-purpose
  or soil-based compost
Strawberry runners (see above)
Straw mulch

1. Choose a large basket or pot that will hold a good volume of compost and water to support the plants. I lined mine with wool that came with an online package, covering it with plastic cut from an old compost bag, and punching a few holes in the base for drainage.

2. Plant your strawberries between 10–20cm (4–8in) apart so they have space to grow, and take care not to bury the crowns – the area where the roots meet the top growth. Firm the compost gently around the stems and water the plants well.

3. I have added a mulch of straw around the plants. This was traditionally used to protect the fruits from soil splash, which can rot them, and it also adds a decorative touch to this basket. Set the basket in a sunny position out of the reach of mice and slugs.

Aftercare
Keep your strawberry plants well watered throughout the growing season, taking care not to wet the fruits, and feed every week when the flowers appear with a high-potassium fertilizer (see pp.56–7). In the first year, experts recommend removing the flowers of everbearers to allow the plants to bulk up and produce a better crop the following year. Plants usually fruit for three or four years before they need replacing (see tip opposite).

CHAPTER 6
AUTUMN

As the temperature and sunlight start to wane, my containers are still packed with colour and interest as I move the autumn performers to the fore, giving sparkling asters, dahlia, and textured grasses pride of place. This is a busy, joyful season for gardeners like me, with lots of planting and propagation to do before the cold winter weather sets in.

PLANTS FOR AUTUMN

As autumn approaches, I shift gear with plants that take over from the summer prima donnas, now on the wane. Leaf interest is important, as deciduous shrubs fire up before their foliage falls later in the season, and there are still plenty of flowers to enjoy, too.

The early days of autumn can remain warm and dry and many summer plants will continue to flower if deadheaded regularly. However, as the weeks pass and temperatures fall, augment them with some of the flowers below and make sure you also have some shrubs and grasses to fill any gaps with their beautiful textures and fiery colours.

Sneezeweed (*Helenium***)**
I grow this hardy perennial in my borders but also plant it in large pots of peat-free compost, so that I can enjoy the orange, red, or yellow cone-shaped blooms up close. These tall, sun-loving plants need staking (see pp.60–1) or try the Chelsea chop, cutting the stems in half in late spring to promote sturdy, bushier growth and more blooms later in early autumn.

Asters (*Aster***;** ***Symphyotrichum***;** ***Kalimeris incisa***;** ***Eurybia***)**
Once known collectively as asters, these late-season perennial flowers are now grouped in various categories and you may find them

Sneezeweed's tall stems of cone-shaped flowers create a focal point.

The daisy-like blooms of asters add pops of colour to an autumn patio display.

listed online and in garden centres as *Aster*, *Eurybia*, *Symphyotrichum*, and *Kalimeris incisa*. Many compact forms are ideal for pots, although I would avoid New York asters (*Symphyotrichum novi-belgii*), which are prone to powdery mildew disease if grown in dry conditions. Asters' daisy-like flowers in shades of pink, red, purple, blue, and white will brighten up autumn pots and they bloom year after year. Their top growth dies down over winter but their seedheads remain, continuing to offer interest during the colder months, before new growth begins again in spring.

Coral bells (*Heuchera*)

These leafy perennials are perfect for growing in pots and hold on to their leaves throughout autumn and winter. New growth then emerges in spring, when the old foliage can be removed. Heucheras are available in a rainbow of foliage colours, from bright green and yellow to red, silver, and dark purple. They also produce tiny, bell-shaped flowers on long, wiry stems for many weeks in summer. Plant them in peat-free multi-purpose or soil-based compost, and divide clumps in spring (see p.25).

Fountain grass (*Pennisetum*)

The fountain grasses are loved for their soft, bottlebrush flowerheads, which appear over arching green or reddish foliage in autumn. Many are evergreen but some are deciduous and will turn brown in winter. I grow these grasses in pots to add texture and movement; their leaves can be so relaxing to watch as they dance in the breeze on the patio. Growing the grasses in containers also means I can place them close to the house in winter for added protection, since they are not reliably hardy. One of my favourites is the red-leaved

Heuchera's frilly, colourful leaves offer invaluable texture.

The red leaves and soft flowerheads of *Pennisetum advena* 'Rubrum' rustle in the breeze.

Pennisetum advena 'Rubrum', with its silver and red flowers. Although it's not fully hardy, it overwinters on my patio next to the house.

Pansy (*Viola*)

Ideal for small pots and seasonal hanging baskets, these useful, diminutive annuals are guaranteed to bring joy when you see the flowers, with their characteristic round faces and central whisker-like markings, beaming back at you. They come in a huge array of colours to suit any container scheme, and flowers range in size from the small violas to larger pansies. You will find trays of pansies for sale at the garden centre in autumn, but it's much cheaper to sow seed in pots of peat-free seed compost in early summer. Growing them yourself will also widen your colour choice, as more varieties are available as seeds (see p.147 for my favourites). Pansies will then bloom well until winter, and may then sulk a little as the temperatures dip, but will then bounce back, saving their best displays for the following spring.

Smoke bush (*Cotinus*)

Varieties of *Cotinus* with purple leaves, such as 'Grace' or *Cotinus coggygria* 'Royal Purple', add leafy background colour to a patio display from spring to summer, before the foliage turns bright red in the autumn, prior to falling. You can only grow this deciduous shrub in a pot when it's young, since it will eventually reach 4m (13ft) or more in height and spread, and will be happier planted in the ground. However, it can remain in a large pot for a number of years. To save money, I also grow smoke bushes from cuttings and pop them in containers on the patio to grow on, until they are ready to go in the border.

Pansies sing from my pots in autumn.

The dark purple leaves of my smoke bush create a leafy backdrop to brighter blooms.

Bowden lily (*Nerine bowdenii*)

This lily is an autumn-flowering bulb, which produces long-lasting pink or white spidery blooms over strappy green foliage. Plant the bulbs in pots in early spring, with their pointed ends just showing above the compost, and keep them in a sheltered spot during the colder months, since they are not fully hardy. They go dormant in summer but when you see new growth emerging, bring them out into a sunny position to flower in autumn. The bulbs are a little pricy but if you can keep them sheltered through the winter, they will flower reliably year after year.

Hebe (*Hebe*)

These much-loved evergreen shrubs look great in pots all year round, but many also flower from summer to early autumn, with spikes of white, purple, or pink blooms, loved by bees. Choose a compact, plain green-leaved variety if you live in a cold area, since these are hardier than the variegated forms, and plant in peat-free soil-based compost, together with a few handfuls of horticultural grit. Place potted hebes in full sun and move them to a sheltered spot over winter, as they dislike cold, wet soil conditions. They have also had a name change and you may find them listed now as *Veronica*.

Heather (*Calluna vulgaris*)

Flowering in autumn, this evergreen shrub will draw many pollinators to your garden with its spikes of small, pink or white flowers. Heathers are drought tolerant and perfect for pots, but they require acidic soil, so remember to plant them in ericaceous compost, and set them in a sunny spot for the best performance. You can also take cuttings from your plants in summer, to make more plants for free.

Hebes' evergreen foliage and summer or early autumn blooms are perfect for pots.

Heathers offer evergreen leaves and white or pink flowers in autumn.

Plants For Autumn

Focus on grasses and sedges

These versatile foliage plants may not be the stars of a patio display but they provide a great back-up chorus. While creating a foil for more colourful performers in spring and summer, grasses then come into their own in autumn, when they produce delicate flowers and seedheads, loved by birds, which look magical with a dusting of frost later in winter. I'm also very sensitive to textures and movement of grasses as they rustle in the wind, which adds another dimension to my container designs.

The main difference between grasses and sedges, as far as gardeners are concerned, is that grasses tend to prefer full sun and free-draining soil, while sedges, including the evergreen *Carex* genus, are happy in some shade and slightly damper soil, although the bronze-leafed types colour best in sun.

Choosing grasses and sedges

There are many grasses and sedges that adapt well to life in a container. My favourites include the tall, tufted hair grass (*Deschampsia cespitosa*); shorter blue-leaved fescues (*Festuca*); fountain grasses (*Pennisetum*), with their bottlebrush-shaped flowers; and the wispy angel hair grass (*Stipa tenuissima*).

The gold and green striped Japanese sedge *Carex oshimensis* 'Evergold' is another good option for a container, and, like most of its cousins, it flowers earlier in summer. While this sedge prefers moist soil, it's not too fussy and will tolerate the drier conditions in a pot.

Planting up

Most grasses and sedges thrive in a pot of peat-free multi-purpose or soil-based compost such as John Innes No. 1. For grasses, you could also mix in a few handfuls of horticultural grit to increase drainage.

Sedges spread via underground stems (rhizomes), and may smother their neighbours in a mixed display, so I always grow them in pots of their own. Ornamental grasses are better behaved and can be combined with plants that enjoy the same conditions, but I prefer growing them on their own, too, as it allows me to pop them into gaps in my displays where just a little foliage is required.

The big split

Dividing clumps of grasses or sedges in late spring or early summer is the easiest way to propagate these plants (see pp.24–5). You can also grow them from seed, and you may find some self-seed, so look out for ready-made babies to plant up in your pots.

Aftercare

Keep pots of grasses and sedges well watered during the growing season. Leave deciduous grasses uncut over winter, since most retain their structure and form, adding a decorative feature at this time of year, while their seeds provide food for birds, and the hollow stems offer shelter and habitats for invertebrates. In early spring, cut all the stems down to the ground. I then use a metal dog's comb to remove the dead stems in the middle of the plant, or just use your fingers. Snip off old or tatty stems on sedge plants at the same time.

Right This graceful angel hair grass decorates my patio all year with its fountains of foliage.

Clockwise from top left: Houseleeks (*Sempervivum*) are hardy and can remain outside in a sheltered spot through autumn and winter; collect seeds of hardy plants to sow now; there's still time to take semi-ripe cuttings of patio plants such as catmint (*Nepeta*); plant prepared hyacinth bulbs for fragrant flowers at Christmas time.

JOBS FOR AUTUMN

The cooler, fresher days of autumn inspire me to get busy and start preparations for next spring, sowing seeds and planting bulbs in pots, while enjoying the fiery foliage colours in the garden as I work. These simple tasks lift my spirits as the days shorten and winter approaches.

There's a lot to do in autumn, as the boxes of spring bulbs I ordered earlier arrive in the post, ready to be planted, and seeds I've collected from the garden need to be sown.

My patio is also full of tender plants such as *Kalanchoe* and aeoniums that offer colour and texture in pots outside during the summer, but are brought back inside to decorate my home as temperatures drop in the autumn. Some succulents, including sedums and houseleeks (*Sempervivum*), are hardy and can stay outside all winter, if sheltered from heavy rain, while slightly tender, summer-flowering plants such as nemesias and snapdragons (*Antirrhinum*) may also survive a mild winter outside in a pot in a sheltered area, but take some cuttings, too, as an insurance policy.

Plant spring bulbs

The main task for autumn is planting spring bulbs in pots, which will burst into bloom the following year. I grow daffodils, hyacinths, grape hyacinths (*Muscari*), little species tulips, alliums, dwarf irises (*Iris reticulata*), and crocuses in containers, but often replant the grape hyacinths and crocuses in the garden after they've flowered, which helps them to recover and bloom again the following year.

You will find bulbs for sale at the garden centre and from online nurseries in early autumn. To save money, look for special offers or buy in bulk from wholesale nurseries (minimum orders may be upwards of 100 bulbs) and share these cheaper bulbs with friends. I also look out for bulbs in late autumn when retailers often reduce them to half price: buying and planting up to Christmas time should not affect next year's display.

Most bulbs thrive in pots of multi-purpose compost, but dwarf irises are best planted in a 50:50 mixture of peat-free compost and horticultural grit, which creates the free-draining conditions they demand. Plant all bulbs at a depth of two to three times the height of the bulb, so a daffodil bulb measuring 5cm (2in) from base to tip is planted it at a depth of at least 10cm (4in). Place your pots in a sheltered area, and cover with prickly stems or a stylish chicken wire cover (see pp.58–9) to prevent squirrels stealing the bulbs.

You can make a bulb lasagne, too, with a collection of bulbs in one pot, with the largest such as narcissus planted at the bottom, and small crocuses nearer the surface. Depending on the varieties you choose, this can offer a succession of blooms from early to late spring.

MONEY-SAVING TIP

Pots of allium bulbs are expensive to buy when in bloom, so I always plant bulbs of the summer-flowering *Allium sphaerocephalon* in trays in autumn, then add them to my containers when the stems appear in spring.

Plant bulbs for festive displays

Tender bulbs such as amaryllis, 'Paper White' narcissi (see pp.160–1) and hyacinths can be planted indoors now to bloom in time for the winter festivities. Also check out the amaryllis project on pp.168–9 for growing advice.

For Christmas-flowering hyacinths, buy bulbs labelled "prepared", which have been heat-treated to make them bloom earlier, in the first weeks of autumn. The cheapest option is to plant them in peat-free multi-purpose compost in pots with drainage holes in the bottom (more expensive bulb fibre is used for pots with no drainage). Plant them close but not touching each other, with the pointed tip just showing above the surface. Cover the pots with a reused black bag and place in a cool shed or garage. When you see roots through the drainage holes and the shoots are 5cm (2in) tall, bring the pots indoors into a cool room and remove the bag. Once the leaves have greened up, move them close to a window in a warmer spot, where they will flower.

Sow seeds to overwinter

Some spring and summer plants are best sown from seed in the autumn (follow the instructions for sowing seed on pp.30–1). My favourites include sweet peas (see the project on pp.134–5), the black-eyed Susan *Thunbergia alata* 'African Sunset', the cup-and-saucer vine (*Cobaea scandens*), and varieties of pot marigold (*Calendula officinalis*). I also collect seed from other flowers in the garden to sow now or store until spring. Try English lavender, astrantias, sweet rocket (*Hesperis matronalis*), dahlias, agapanthus, opium poppies, verbena, love-in-a-mist (*Nigella*), *Cerinthe major*, and bunny tails (*Lagurus ovatus*), all of which perform well in pots. While seed bought from seed merchants is guaranteed to produce the flower size, shape, and colour described on the packet or website, sowing from harvested seeds is more of a gamble, and the plants that arise from them may not look exactly like the original plants because they've reverted to resemble the species, but it's fun to see what will pop up. For example, most of my dahlia seeds make plants with yellow flowers, but I love experimenting in this way and it's free, so nothing is lost in the process.

Continue to take cuttings

There's still time to take cuttings from your patio plants, including tender types such as pelargoniums and fuchsias, as well as hardier perennials, including *Nepeta* and salvias. Try semi-ripe cuttings or pop a few stems in water (see pp.26–9 for methods).

Plant seasonal pots

I don't want to look at bare compost all winter, and enjoy making beautiful displays that will offer interest from autumn until spring. Use cuttings taken from evergreen shrubs (see pp.26–9), together with sedges such as *Carex*, and pansies and violas. Try adding some spring bulbs such as dwarf narcissus and grape hyacinths (*Muscari*) in a layer under the evergreens, grasses, and pansies. These will then pop up like a floral surprise present in spring, pushing their way through the gaps between the other plants.

Stop feeding

As growth slows down in late autumn and many plants take their annual rest, it's time to stop feeding them. Too much fertilizer now can also stimulate new, soft growth that is more vulnerable frost damage. Plants in containers also need less watering as temperatures cool and autumn rain returns.

Taking cuttings of evergreen shrubs such as *Pittosporum* in late summer or early autumn will provide you with free plants for your container displays the following year.

SIMPLY SWEET PEAS

If you follow me on social media, you will know that I adore sweet peas, their climbing stems of scented flowers creating long-lasting focal points in summer and autumn, all for the cost of a packet of seeds.

Sweet peas (*Lathyrus odoratus*) flower from early summer to early autumn, but are best sown in the autumn before, germinating and growing in the proceeding months to make sturdy little plants that you can add to pots in late spring.

There are thousands of sweet pea varieties, in almost every colour under the sun, with new cultivars appearing every year. The old-fashioned types, known as "grandifloras", have small, high fragrant flowers, while modern grandifloras produce larger flowers on strong stems, also with an amazing scent. I adore the maroon and purple 'Early Grey'; 'Mr P', with purple flowers; and the Frilly Series, which have frilly petals. Other favourites are the cream 'Cathy'; 'Lisa Marie', with its raspberry-ripple flowers; and the pink, purple and cream 'Fire and Ice'. The only old-fashioned one I grow is 'Matucana', the most fragrant variety of all, which, as a neurodivergent person, simply takes me to heaven.

You will need
Sweet pea seed
Peat-free seed compost
Root trainers or deep pots
Tray
Peat-free multi-purpose compost
Plant support and large pot

1. In autumn, soak the seeds overnight. Then line a food tray or box with a wet kitchen paper towel, place the seeds on top and cover them with another layer of towel. Set on a warm windowsill, keep the towels moist, and the seeds usually germinate within two days.

2. Fill root trainers or deep pots with moist, peat-free seed compost and add two pre-germinated seeds in each, at a depth of about 2.5cm (1in). Stand the pots in a tray with drainage holes in a sheltered spot outside. Add a few twiggy supports for the young seedlings to climb.

3. In early spring, give the seedlings a boost by placing them on a tray (with drainage holes) filled with a 5cm (2in) layer of multi-purpose compost. This delivers more nutrients to the roots, which grow into the rich compost and shoot up. Also feed now with nitrogen-rich fertilizer (see pp.56–7).

4. In late spring, fill a large pot with peat-free multi-purpose compost and install the support, wedging it in so it won't topple in wind. Plant the sweet peas around the edge, with their twiggy supports. Water well and leave them to climb the support and flower.

Aftercare
Keep plants well watered, and cut the flowers regularly, which will prompt more flowering stems to form. Feed weekly from late spring with a comfrey or potassium-rich fertilizer.

1.

2.

3.

4.

Kohlrabi serves two roles in pots on my patio, creating a decorative foliage plant at first, and then a delicious crop when the stems swell into little round edible balls.

VERSATILE KOHLRABI

You may not be familiar with kohlrabi since these little cabbage-like veg aren't widely available in the shops, but they are easy to grow from seed and have a dual purpose on a patio, providing an ornamental leafy plant at first and then a delicious crop in summer and autumn.

My family in Poland has always grown kohlrabi, where the sweet swollen stems are often eaten raw as a snack, and growing it on my patio helps to connect me to my homeland. These nutritious little balls taste like mild turnips, and can also be grated for use in coleslaw, or lightly steamed or sautéed.

You can choose varieties with green, white, or purple skins, but I tend to grow the latter because they have two uses, the beautiful blue-green foliage and purple stems creating a pretty patio display, followed by tasty crops.

Sow seeds of purple kohlrabi from spring to summer for a midsummer harvest and from mid- to late summer for autumn harvests. The stems can also be stored in autumn in a cool place for use in winter, although you probably won't have enough to keep if you're only growing them in pots.

A packet of seeds costs just a few pence, and by sowing small batches every couple of weeks, you can harvest them over many weeks.

You will need
Packet of kohlrabi seeds
Small recycled pots
Peat-free seed compost
Deep, decorative pots
Peat-free multi-purpose compost

1. From spring to late summer sow two seeds in small, recycled pots of peat-free seed compost to a depth of 1cm (½in). You can keep them outside, since the plants are hardy, but some protection from slugs and snails is helpful – I place my seedlings on a table.

2. Germination should occur within two weeks. Remove the weakest seedling once they are 2.5–5cm (1–2in) tall and leave the remaining one to grow on for a few more weeks to establish a good root system. Keep them in light shade and water well to prevent the compost drying out, which can slow growth and produce woody stems.

3. When the seedlings have a few sets of leaves and you can see roots through the pot's drainage holes, transplant them into larger pots of peat-free multi-purpose compost.

4. After a couple of months, the base of the stem will begin to swell into a little round ball. Harvest the crops when they are between a golf ball and tennis ball in size.

Aftercare
Keep the compost moist to prevent the stems from becoming woody. Plants should not need feeding if grown in fresh peat-free compost, which already contains sufficient nutrients. Cabbage whitefly can be a problem so check plants regularly for signs of their eggs and caterpillars and remove them promptly.

SHADY CONTAINER

Some of my favourite plants are the shy, retiring sorts that prefer life in the shade, and many are evergreens that will withstand harsh autumn and winter weather. Try this beautiful display for long-lasting interest.

This selection of evergreen plants offers colour and texture whatever the weather, while the pops of flower colour add seasonal highlights. All the plants will endure year after year, except for the pansies, which are annuals and will start flowering in autumn, offer a few blooms in winter, and then give their best show in spring.

The necklace vine is only hardy to -5°C (23°F) but survives most winters on my sheltered patio. I also root a few stems in water (see p.29) each autumn to generate more plants and as insurance against losses. I also root ivy stems in a pot of compost or the ground, which deliver new plants for next year's winter pots. The *Carex* spreads, too, if planted in the ground in spring, giving me more plants to lift and divide for future autumn and winter displays.

You will need
Large pot
Peat-free multi-purpose compost
Heucheras with colourful leaves (I used 'Lime Marmalade' and 'Forever Purple')
Sedge (*Carex oshimensis* 'Everest')
Ivy (*Hedera helix*)
Necklace vine (*Muehlenbeckia complexa*) (optional)
Pansies (*Viola*)
White ivy-leaved cyclamen (*Cyclamen hederifolium* var. *hederifolium* f. *albiflorum*)

1. To save money on compost, place an old plastic pot upside down in the bottom of the container, and fill around it with compost. Alternatively, fill the bottom of the pot with topsoil collected from mole hills, if you have any. Leave a gap of about 7.5cm (3in) between the compost and pot rim.

2. Water all the plants thoroughly. Then start to fill the container, adding the sedge and heucheras in the middle, and the trailing necklace vine and ivy around the sides.

3. Finally squeeze the pansies and cyclamen in the gaps to finish off the display, making sure that they will receive enough light and are not hidden at the back in the shade.

4. Stand in a sheltered spot, out of strong winds, and water well. Also raise the pot on feet (see pp.58–9) to increase drainage.

Aftercare
This winter pot will not need feeding until spring when you can add an organic fertilizer such as comfrey or any plant-based potassium-rich fertilizer. This encourages the pansies and heucheras to flower and thrive, if you are planning to keep the plants in the pot for another year. I rarely water winter pots unless there is an exceptionally long, dry period, but then start watering about once a week from spring, when the plants are growing again.

BARRELS OF BLOOMS

One of my favourite flowers is the Mexican fleabane, a beautiful little perennial with daisy-like flowers that turn from white to pink as they age. I harvest and sow the seeds from existing plants to save money.

The cheapest way to dress up your patio with a flower-filled barrel is to collect seed from existing Mexican fleabane (*Erigeron karvinskianus*) anytime between early summer and late autumn. To harvest the seed, observe the seedheads early in the morning to see which are almost ready to burst. By midday, they will turn slightly fluffy and the seed can be collected by tapping them gently into a paper bag. Then tip the seeds out on to a piece of paper to dry. Alternatively, you may find seedlings scattered around the garden that you can collect (see pp.32–3), or – if you don't have a plant already – simply buy the seeds.

I've planted mine in wooden half barrels to create a flowery edging next to the house, but these little plants suit any size of pot, and are very drought-tolerant, although they need a site in full sun for the best flower show.

You will need
Wooden half barrel
Electric drill, 25mm (1in) spade wood drill bit, and dust mask
Peat-free multi-purpose compost mixed with used compost or molehill topsoil
Erigeron karvinskianus seed

1. Sow the seeds in trays of seed compost, covering them with a fine sprinkling of compost, as they need light to germinate. Set them outside in a sheltered spot and keep the compost moist, but not wet.

2. When the seedlings are about 10cm (4in) in height, prepare your barrel. Wearing a dust mask, turn it over and make four large holes in the base using the electric drill and drill bit. This is an important step, since the barrels are watertight, and the plants will drown in waterlogged compost with no drainage.

3. Fill the barrel to about 5cm (2in) from the top with a mix of peat-free multi-purpose compost mixed with used compost, if you have any, to save money. Or set a few old plant pots upside down in the bottom of the barrel and fill in around them. If you have moles, you can use soil collected from the molehills to fill the bottom third for free!

4. I have planted three seedlings in a standard size barrel, 65cm (26in) in diameter, spacing them 20–25cm (8–10in) apart. Water them in, and keep moist. When planted in early summer, the barrels will soon fill with flowers that will continue to bloom until late autumn, or even through winter if they are in a relatively warm, sheltered spot.

Aftercare
Apply homemade comfrey fertilizer (see pp.56–7), or a high-potassium feed from the garden centre, once a week from spring to late summer, to give the plants a boost. And lightly cut back the plant stems in early spring to make them bushier and more floriferous.

1.

2.

3.

4.

STORING HERBS

My patio is always full of herbs in pots, but come the autumn my attention turns to overwintering my plants and storing the tasty leaves to bring the taste of summer to my winter and early spring dishes.

Growing herbs in containers on your patio, balcony, or window box is very easy, since these flavoursome plants are generally drought-tolerant and pest- and disease-free.

My favourites for pots include basil and dwarf varieties of dill, which I grow from seed sown indoors in early spring. These tender annuals must be protected until all risk of frost has passed, after which plant them outside in pots of peat-free multi-purpose compost in full sun. Parsley is another herb that's easy to raise from seed, and because it is hardy the seedlings can go outside earlier in the spring in sun or a little shade.

Sun-loving shrubby herbs that can be kept outside in pots all year round include thyme, rosemary, and sage. Plant them in a 4:1 mix of peat-free compost and horticulture grit and feed annually in spring with an all-purpose, organic plant-based fertilizer. You can also take cuttings from these herbs in spring or summer (see pp.26–9), and overwinter them indoors on a windowsill.

The leaves of herbs should not be harvested in winter, when plant growth is slow or halts altogether, so follow these steps to store them from summer to early autumn.

Freezing herbs

Most herbs freeze really well, retaining their flavour for six months or more. On a warm, sunny morning, remove the leaves you want to store and freeze them whole in a freezer bag or container, labelled with the name of the herb and the date. Alternatively, chop up the herbs and freeze them in ice-cube trays topped up with water. You can then pop a cube into soup or a drink for a quick burst of herby flavour.

Drying stems

I also dry some of the shrubby herbs such as rosemary and sage, which fills my kitchen with fragrance. Tie the stems of the herbs together with soft twine and hang them up in a warm, dry, well-ventilated place, out of direct sunlight. For smaller-leaved herbs such as thyme, which may drop their foliage as they dry, set the stems on a tray lined with kitchen towels. When the herbs have dried, remove the leaves and store them in airtight containers in a cool, dark place.

....

MANAGING MINT

I always recommend growing mint in a container, since it's very vigorous and tends to overwhelm its neighbours when grown in the ground, often taking over a whole bed. If you want to grow this spreading herb in a mixed container with others, plunge the plant, still in its original pot, into the compost. Some roots will find their way out through the drainage holes in the bottom, but they will be restricted and won't smother everything else in the container.

....

Clockwise from top left: Growing a range of herbs in pots provides leaves from spring to early autumn; harvest your herbs in the morning and chop up the leaves or freeze them whole; I also dry a few shrubby herbs such as thyme and sage in the kitchen; add the herbs to a labelled container or bag and pop in the freezer.

Clockwise from top left: After sowing your pansies, transplant the seedlings into modules when they have a couple of sets of leaves; when seedlings have put on some growth in autumn, plant in their final container; search for forget-me-not seedlings and plant them up in autumn; group the containers for a long season of interest.

AUTUMN-TO-SPRING POTS

Autumn is a time to celebrate the bright seasonal colours but I also use this time to plan for spring – planting pansies, searching for forget-me-not seedlings to pot up, and adding evergreens to containers, which all provide a long season of interest from now until next year.

I start planning my spring containers the previous summer, when I sow my pansies (*Viola × wittrockiana*). These will then start flowering from mid-autumn, and overwinter outside to bloom more abundantly as the temperatures rise the following year. There are hundreds of colours to choose from and my favourites are the dark black varieties and rich burgundies, purples, and pinks that look gorgeous with daffodils, and the frilly petalled Frizzle Sizzle series.

In autumn, I also hunt for forget-me-not (*Myosotis sylvatica*) seedlings, which I find all over the garden and in pots (see pp.32–3). To add height and structure, I've included the spurge *Euphorbia characias* 'Black Pearl'. This compact shrub has dark grey-green leaves and spikes of small, green-yellow flowers with purple eyes in spring. I grow it in the garden and root stems in water in summer (see p.29).

Sow pansies

From early to late summer, sow pansy seeds in pots or trays of moist seed compost, as instructed on the packet. Keep in a sheltered area, protected from slugs and snails. When the seedlings have a few leaves, transplant them into individual pots. Keep the seedlings moist and when roots have filled the pots, plant them in a decorative pot filled with peat-free multi-purpose compost.

Plant forget-me-not seedlings

Meanwhile, look around the garden and other pots for forget-me-not seedlings. Water if the ground is dry, then remove them with a trowel, popping them into a tray before transplanting them into a pretty container.

Add the spurge

Finally, fill a pot to about 5cm (2in) from the rim with peat-free soil-based compost and plant your *Euphorbia* cuttings (or buy a plant). Remember to wear gloves when handling *Euphorbia*. Then simply group your pots together for a colourful combo.

Aftercare

Keep the pots watered, and deadhead pansies regularly to keep the plants blooming from early spring to summer. I also cut back the stems in early summer to further prolong flowering. Remove old flower stems from the *Euphorbia* when the blooms have faded.

MONEY-SAVING TIP

Pansies are also easy to grow from cuttings. If you buy a hybrid and wish to grow it again, take cuttings and root them in pots or a glass of water (see p.29) in spring or summer, to produce a plant identical to the parent.

LEAFY TRANSITION

Taking leaf cuttings is one of the easiest propagation methods and can create lots of new plants from just one parent. Here, I am propagating the paddle plant *Kalanchoe thyrsiflora*, which decorates my patio in summer and makes a beautiful houseplant in autumn and winter.

Some plants just shout "Look at me!" and the paddle plant (*Kalanchoe thyrsiflora*) is a prime example. Its rosette of huge, fleshy, grey-green leaves turn red in the summer as they mature, adding drama to any summer container display, and although it is not hardy, it doubles as a wonderful houseplant when temperatures fall from autumn to spring.

This beauty is also a favourite because it's so easy to propagate from leaf cuttings. Each leaf will form a new plant in just a few months, with very little fuss, making this the perfect project for beginners.

You will need
Paddle plant (*Kalanchoe thyrsiflora*)
Small pots or trays
Peat-free succulent or cuttings compost
Horticultural grit
Chopstick or dibber
Larger container with drainage holes

1. You can take these cuttings all year round, but I have the most success from summer to early autumn. First remove healthy, mature leaves from around the edges of the plant, so the parent doesn't look too bare, gently tugging them to the left and right to loosen them.

2. Then pop your leaves into a glass of tap water, so just the lower stems are submerged. Keep them out of direct sun, either outside in summer or indoors in autumn or winter. Change the water when it looks cloudy, washing out the glass first. Roots will soon develop on the stems.

3. Fill small pots or seed trays with succulent compost or a 4:1 mix of cuttings compost and horticultural grit. Using a chopstick, make a small hole at the side of the pot and insert a rooted leaf into the compost, firming around it gently. Repeat with more leaves, making sure that they are not touching. Water the compost carefully, ensuring the leaves do not get wet.

4. Keep the cuttings in a warm, bright area indoors, and water the compost only when the surface feels dry – overwatering may cause the leaves to rot. When the pot is filled with roots, transfer each cutting into its own pot, using the compost and grit mix above.

Aftercare
Set plants outside in a sunny spot in late spring after the frosts, but bring them indoors in autumn as soon as night-time temperatures fall. Water from spring to summer when the top of the compost feels dry, and apply a half dose of cactus fertilizer in summer – I often forget to feed mine and they still thrive! Water less frequently in winter, applying just enough to prevent the leaves from shrivelling.

1.

2.

3.

4.

CHAPTER 7
WINTER

The coldest season of the year can be one of the happiest for me. While much of the garden is asleep, there are still pockets of joy to be found in the winter months, with pots of seasonal foliage and flowers on my patio and indoors. I also use this quiet time to take stock of what the year has delivered – plants that have been successful and those that haven't done so well, while looking forward to the treasures yet to come.

PLANTS FOR WINTER

I shrug off the winter blues with a patio packed with colour and interest, placing pots of flowers and foliage where I can see them through the windows from the warmth of my home. Here are a few of my favourites, which lift my displays during these cold, dark months.

Evergreens are the mainstay of my winter container display, with hardy shrubs and ferns such as the soft shield fern (*Polystichum setiferum*), skimmias, sweet box, and spurges creating the backbone of my displays. To these, I add bold winter flowers, including hellebores (see pp.156–7) and snowdrops (see pp.164–5), and the deciduous grasses *Stipa tenuissima* and *Stipa lessingiana* that keep their structure in winter, creating an eye-catching combination of colours and textures. I also leave some of my summer and autumn flowers such as *Echinacea* and asters to form seedheads that provide additional interest and overwintering habitats for insects.

Ivy (*Hedera helix*)

Set off your winter pots with a frill of ivy trailing around the edges. Nothing could be easier to grow, and you can take a few cuttings from the stems to grow on for future displays or to give away to friends. Be aware that when

Ivy cuttings root rapidly in spring, and will be ready to plant in pots for winter.

The pink buds of *Skimmia* plants offer winter colour before opening in spring.

planted in the ground, ivy can take over large areas of the garden, although it is a wonderful plant for wildlife, offering food for pollinators and nesting sites for birds. However, keeping it in a container restricts its growth, and I love growing different varieties on my patio.

Skimmia (*Skimmia*)

These shade-tolerant evergreen shrubs are perfect for winter pots, offering a display of glossy green leaves and heads of pink or green buds that open to reveal small, white flowers later in spring. These shrubs are "dioecious", which means their reproductive parts are on different plants: the males have the largest, showiest buds and flowerheads, while the females produce red berries from late summer, after the flowers have faded, if pollinated by a male form growing nearby. Plant skimmias in pots of ericaceous compost.

Japanese sedge (*Carex*)

Perfect for winter pots, variegated sedges, such as *Carex oshimensis* 'Evergold' with pale yellow stripes, or 'Everest', which sports white stripes, create a splash of colour at this time of year. These compact evergreens grow to about 30cm (12in) in height and spread, and are very easy to care for in containers. Set them in a sunny or partially shaded site, and keep them watered from spring to autumn. They spread quickly and can be divided (see pp.24–5) in spring to make more plants for free.

Sweet box (*Sarcococca*)

The small, glossy evergreen leaves of sweet box create a simple, textured backdrop for seasonal flower displays throughout the year, but it is in winter, when their little white flowers burst into bloom and release the most intoxicating scent, that they really make an impact. These

This variegated *Carex* is ideal for decorating winter pots.

Sweet box comes into its own now, when its tiny scented flowers unfurl.

compact shrubs are happy growing in large pots of peat-free soil-based compost, and my favourites include the free-flowering *Sarcococca confusa* and *Sarcococca hookeriana* var. *digyna* 'Purple Stem', whose white and pink flowers appear on reddish-purple stems. Take semi-ripe cuttings (see p.26) of both to make new plants for free.

Japanese aralia (*Fatsia japonica*)
The Japanese aralia is often sold as a houseplant but this medium-sized evergreen shrub is actually hardy and makes a dramatic statement in a container outside. The large, glossy, lobed leaves look almost tropical and are joined by cream, spherical flowerheads, which are loved by bees, in early autumn. Plant it in a peat-free soil-based compost such as John Innes No. 3 and set it in a shady spot – it's even happy in the deep shade under a tree.

Spurge (*Euphorbia*)
Many euphorbias are evergreen, their stems of slim, fingerlike leaves offering colour and texture in winter, while the flowerheads are a bonus in spring. Good options for containers include *Euphorbia characias* 'Black Pearl', with its dark-eyed green flowers, the purple-leaved *Euphorbia* 'Miners Merlot', and *Euphorbia* 'Ascot Petite', which has dark foliage and bright yellow blooms. The stems contain a toxic latex-like sap that can cause temporary blindness if it gets into your eyes, so wear gloves when handling these plants and keep them away from children and pets.

Fortune's spindle (*Euonymus fortunei*)
The variegated evergreen leaves of this hardy shrub provide sparkling highlights on a winter patio, terrace, or balcony. You can choose between gold or silver variegations, depending

Use the fingerlike leaves of *Euphorbia characias* 'Black Pearl' to dress up a winter patio

Fortune's spindle is loved for its sparkling evergreen foliage.

on your colour preference, and some take on pinkish tints in autumn. Plant this spindle in a peat-free soil-based compost such as John Innes No. 3 and set it in a sunny or partly shaded area. Young shrubs sold as winter bedding are much cheaper than mature plants.

Mondo grass (*Ophiopogon planiscapus* 'Kokuryū')

The glossy, black leaves of this grass-like evergreen perennial look fabulous in a terracotta or colourful glazed pot in winter. It also produces small, purplish flowers in summer, followed by glossy, black berries that last through the winter. This little treasure reaches about 20cm (8in) in height, and is best planted in peat-free soil-based or multi-purpose compost. Set it in a sunny or partly shaded spot and pair it with some snowdrops for a dramatic black and white winter display.

Amaryllis (*Hippeastrum*)

While amaryllis are not hardy, they are among my favourite winter flowers for the home and grow easily from large bulbs, which are planted indoors in the autumn (see pp.168–9). Buy a few different varieties for a spectacular, colourful display of huge, trumpet-shaped blooms from mid- to late winter.

Hydrangea seedheads

One of my favourite winter container plants is actually my hydrangea, which produces the most beautiful buff-coloured seedheads at this time of year. The seedheads protect the buds, which develop below them on the stems, from frost and should be left in place until mid-spring. Other lovely winter seedheads to enjoy include grasses such as *Stipa* (see p.128) and *Miscanthus* (see p.37), *Echinacea* (see p.90), and asters (see pp.124–5).

Amaryllis are tender plants that decorate the windowsills in my home in winter.

The textured seedheads of hydrangeas are a match for any flower.

Plants For Winter

Clockwise from top left: Removing the leaves before hellebores, such as this *Helleborus* 'Angel Glow', open helps to prevent disease; one of my own homegrown plants sown from seed; the green flowers of *Helleborus argutifolius* bloom for months from midwinter; this beauty has no name but popped up from a seedling I found.

Focus on hellebores

Hellebores are evergreen perennials that flower from early to late winter, sometimes longer, and offer months of interest on a patio. Displaying them in pots on a table or chair allows you to inspect the exquisite nodding flowers at close range and appreciate their colours and patterns more easily.

Plant them in a peat-free soil-based compost such as John Innes No. 3 and set them in light shade – most can be stored out of the way at the back of a container display after flowering. Keep the compost moist but not wet; adding a mulch of bark chips over the surface will help to keep them hydrated for longer during hot, dry periods in the summer.

Colours and forms

One of the first hellebores to flower is the Christmas rose (*Helleborus niger*). Producing pure white or pink-flushed white flowers over dark green, leathery leaves at Christmas time or just after, this beautiful plant is best kept in a pot in a sheltered spot, so that heavy rain or frost won't damage the blooms.

The popular Lenten roses (*Helleborus × hybridus*) are next, flowering over a long period from midwinter to early spring. You will find a large selection of these colourful hybrids to buy online or at the garden centre.

The holly-leaved hellebore (*Helleborus argutifolius*) looks a little different, with its large, dramatic, spiny foliage and pale green flowers, which again last for a few months, often opening around New Year and blooming until mid-spring. These Mediterranean plants prefer a little more sun than other hellebores.

Another beauty that grows particularly well in the shade is the stinking hellebore (*Helleborus foetidus*). Don't be put off by the name, however, since it only refers to the slim green leaves that smell when crushed, while the odourless dainty, pale green flowers bloom for a long period from late winter to spring.

Plants for free

For a money-saving gardener, there is just one problem with hellebores and that is their cost. However, most self-seed freely and you will find seedlings scattered around the parent to dig up and add to your patio display. The babies often don't come true to type, and can produce flower colours unlike the parent, but that's the best bit. I love surprises and have collected many wonderful hellebores for free in this way. You can also harvest the seeds from the plants at the beginning of summer.

Aftercare

As my hellebores start to flower, I remove all the foliage to prevent the plants contracting hellebore leaf spot, which weakens the plant. You don't have to do this if the foliage on your plants looks healthy, but I find that even if they are not diseased, the leaves can look a bit scrappy at this time of the year and removing them allows the flowers to shine. Keep potted plants watered during dry periods and set them in shade in the summer. A slow-release organic fertilizer, such as those containing seaweed, applied to plants in pots in early spring and again in late summer will help to keep them healthy.

While few plants can be sown in winter, microgreens germinate easily all year round on a windowsill indoors, delivering nutritious shoots for salads and sandwiches.

JOBS FOR WINTER

Cold temperatures and low light levels prompt many herbaceous plants to seek refuge underground in winter, but I see the garden as a theatre with a show that must go on, with potted evergreens to cheer me up, and little jobs that need doing to remind me of treasures yet to come.

I catch up on spring bulb planting during the first weeks of winter, adding money-saving buys that are often available now (see p.131). This makes it a good time to take a punt on flowers you may not have grown before, such as the tall, snowdrop-like, spring snowflake *Leucojum vernum* or an unusual fritillary.

Winter is like a propagation festival: I continue to harvest seeds from the garden and take hardwood cuttings from shrubs and roses (see p.26). Now is also the time to stop feeding your plants.

Prune potted roses

If you're growing roses in containers, give them a prune in late winter. Take out old stems that didn't flower well the previous summer, and any that are crossing each other. Then shorten others by about a third to a healthy bud. Use sharp, clean secateurs and make your cuts just above a bud or leaf joint. Leave newly planted dwarf and patio roses for a year or two before pruning them.

Cut back grasses

Leave deciduous grasses such as *Miscanthus* and *Stipa* unpruned in winter, when their stems add texture to a display. Then, in late winter or early spring, cut them back to 10–15cm (4–6in) above the surface. I run a dog comb through the cut stems to remove any remaining old growth – a very satisfying task.

Root stems in water

A lovely mindful job to do in winter is to propagate a few herbs, bought from the supermarket or collected from the garden. Pop stems of rosemary, mint, sage, and even basil (an annual plant, normally best grown from seeds, but it will also root in winter) in water (see p.29). I find watching the new roots develop very uplifting and especially powerful on a grey wintry day.

Grow microgreens

I have always grown a few microgreens, even as a little girl when we only had cress seeds to enjoy. Now we're spoiled for choice, with broccoli, spinach, beetroot, and chard, to name a few. Simply spread the seeds out on a few sheets of damp kitchen paper or a layer of compost in a shallow food tray. Set in a light, warm place indoors, misting them regularly until they germinate. Snip off the microgreen stems when they reach about 5cm (2in).

Shelter your drought-lovers

Some plants do not like wet winter weather – lavender, agapanthus, hardy succulents, and other drought-loving plants, in particular. To save them rotting in damp compost, place their pots under the eaves of your house, or another spot that's sheltered from rain, and set them on pot feet (see p.58–9). Pop them back in their original positions when spring arrives.

THE GIFT OF DAFFODILS

Every autumn I plant paperwhite daffodil bulbs in pots to flower indoors over the festive period and give away as gifts. These flowers have an intoxicating scent and you can keep the bulbs for a few years.

Paperwhites are daffodils from the southern Mediterranean region, and while most are not completely hardy and are only suitable for growing outside in mild areas, they make beautiful indoor displays and can be forced to flower during the winter festive season.

These beautiful narcissi produce clusters of small, white flowers with a wonderful perfume and grow from dry bulbs planted in autumn. There are a few different varieties to choose from, but all take from six to ten weeks after planting to flower indoors, so decide when you want them to bloom and calculate when to start this project.

You will need
Pot with drainage holes in the base
Peat-free multi-purpose compost
Paperwhites such as *Narcissus* 'Paper White', 'Cragford', 'Erlicheer', or 'Inbal'
Moss (optional)
Tray or saucer
Twiggy stems to decorate

1. In early autumn, place some crocks over the drainage holes at the bottom of a container, then half fill it with peat-free compost.

2. Plant the narcissus bulbs close together, but not touching, with the pointed ends facing up. Add more compost, so that the tips of the bulbs are just below the surface.

3. To make the display prettier while I wait for the flowers to emerge, I cover the surface with moss gathered from my lawn, and have also added an *Echeveria* offset (see p.112).

4. Stand the pot on a saucer and water well. Set on a warm, sunny windowsill, watering when the top of the compost feels dry. When the stems emerge, add some twiggy stems – I've used corkscrew hazel (*Corylus avellana* 'Contorta') – or sticks found on walks, for decoration and to help support the flowers. As the daffodils appear, I set the display in a cool room or outside close to the back door, if the weather is not too cold, to greet me as I come into the house.

Aftercare
Remove the faded blooms after flowering, and leave the plants in a sunny spot indoors, to allow the leaves to photosynthesize and feed the bulbs. Alternatively, plant the hardier types such as *Narcissus* 'Cragford', 'Erlicheer', and 'Inbal' in the ground after flowering, where they will recharge well (add a marker so you know where they are), and dig them up in autumn to replant in pots.

For more tender types, such as 'Paper White', remove the bulbs after the foliage has withered, leave to dry, and store in paper bags in a cool place over the summer. Plant those that are still firm the following autumn.

1.

2.

3.

4.

GROW A CHRISTMAS TREE FROM SEED

No artificial tree can match the scent and colour of a real Christmas tree and while they are quite expensive to buy, you can grow baby plants from seed for almost no cost, but you will need a little patience.

The winter festive season is a wonderful time of year, when many people like to decorate their homes with Christmas trees. As an environmentally conscious gardener, I prefer real trees to artificial ones, and save money by buying them as saplings from a Christmas Tree nursery, growing them on in pots of peat-free soil-based compost.

If you want a larger tree to keep year after year, buy one labelled "pot-grown" and then repot it in early spring in peat-free soil-based compost, such as John Innes No. 2. Feed both saplings and older trees with an all-purpose fertilizer in spring and keep them well watered.

A few years ago, I also tried sowing seeds from pine cones found in the park. This is a project for patient gardeners as the seed can be slow to germinate and plants take a few years to reach a usable size, but it's fun and free.

You will need
Pine cones
Peat-free seed compost
Reused plant pots
Peat-free soil-based compost

1. On a dry day in autumn, collect closed pine cones, which will not yet have released their seeds, from the ground. Take them home and place in a warm spot to encourage them to open. Then shake the cones into your hand to release the seeds. Put them in a glass of water and use seeds that sink, which will be more likely to germinate.

2. The seeds then need a cold period to trigger germination, a process known as stratification. First, soak the seed in water for 24 hours, then drain, before placing the moist seeds in a bag in the freezer for 6–8 weeks. Remove the seeds and sow in small pots of seed compost. Sow on the surface and cover with a fine sprinkling of compost, since the seeds need light to germinate. Set the pots in a cool, bright room or sheltered spot outside, and keep the compost moist. Germination can take a few weeks up to a few months.

3. When the seedlings' roots have filled their pots, repot into larger containers of peat-free soil-based compost, such as John Innes No. 2.

4. Grow the trees on in full sun. In winter, decorate as desired to showcase in your home.

Aftercare
Keep your trees well watered and add an all-purpose organic fertilizer in spring. Repot the trees in winter when you see roots growing out of the drainage holes. Baby trees will form in about two years, but they will take five to ten years to achieve the size of bought trees.

YEAR-AFTER-YEAR SNOWDROPS

The dainty white flowers of snowdrops peeping out of a moss-edged pot lifts my spirits in late winter, when the garden is looking quite bare. To save money, I keep these little beauties going year after year.

We all need something to look forward to as winter drags on and – for me – it's my snowdrops (*Galanthus*), their little nodding heads heralding in spring. These elegant bulbs are best bought and planted after flowering, with their leaves still intact. You will find lots of different varieties for sale from specialist nurseries "in the green", as it's known, but you will also discover that they are not cheap. However, since many people don't realize that it's best to plant them after flowering, you may find potted snowdrops with faded blooms in the reduced area at the garden centre.

I always include snowdrops in containers close to the house where I can see their pretty, shy faces from my window or when I walk outside, but they struggle to survive their summer dormant period when kept in pots all year round. The compost is too dry for them and they are far more likely to bloom again if you can plant them in the garden to recharge and then dig them up to add to pots again the following year.

You will need
Snowdrops (*Galanthus*)
Trowel and tray
Reused plastic plant pot
Peat-free multi-purpose compost
Decorative pot with drainage holes
Moss (purchased or harvested from a lawn)

1. Plant snowdrops in spring in a cool, shady spot in the garden, incorporating some garden compost into the soil first to help prevent it drying out. Also add a mulch of compost over the surface. Mark where they are, since they will disappear underground in summer, but keep watering throughout summer, to help the bulbs establish.

2. When you see buds emerging in winter, dig up a clump with a trowel, taking care not to damage the roots or delicate stems. Place them in a tray.

3. Fill the reused plant pot with peat-free compost and plant the snowdrops at the same depth they were growing at in the soil.

4. Pop the pot into a decorative container. Add a little moss around the edges of the pot and water well, before placing it in a slightly shaded area on the patio.

Aftercare
Water the pot a little during dry winters to keep the flowers looking fresh. Once they have faded, simply replant them in their original position in the garden to grow on and naturalize. In this way, I now have carpets of snowdrops to enjoy both in the garden and on my patio each year.

1.

2.

3.

4.

1.

2.

3.

4.

AMAZING AMARYLLIS

I always find a place in my home for amaryllis each year and love watching their dull brown bulbs transform into spectacular trumpet-shaped flowers during some of the darkest days of the year.

My grandmother and mother in Poland always grew amaryllis (*Hippeastrum*) and it's a family tradition that I really enjoy continuing with my boys. The huge flowers come in colours ranging from dark red and pink to peachy-orange and white, with many sporting stripes and patterned petals.

To the uninitiated, the huge bulbs look challenging and many people don't buy them simply because they are unsure how to grow them. Well, it couldn't be easier, and all you need is a pot and some compost to get started. Plant your bulbs six to eight weeks before you would like them to bloom.

You will need
Pots with drainage holes, a little larger than the bulbs
Peat-free multi-purpose compost
Amaryllis bulbs
Moss (optional)
Pine cones (optional)

1. Add a layer of peat-free multi-purpose compost to the bottom of the pot. I've used a terracotta pot, but I also plant them in old tin cans, with holes punched in the base. Place the amaryllis bulb on top of the compost, with the pointed end facing up.

2. Check that once it is planted, the top third to a half of the bulb will be above the surface, and add or remove compost accordingly. When the bulb is at the right level, fill in around it with more compost. Water lightly, avoiding the bulb.

3. I've added some moss raked from the lawn over the compost to help keep it damp, and a few pine cones for decoration. Set the pot on a warm, sunny windowsill indoors and keep the compost damp, but not wet.

4. Stems will soon emerge from the top of the bulb. Keep turning the pot to prevent the stems leaning towards the light. When blooms appear 6–8 weeks after planting, move to a cool spot to prolong flowering.

Aftercare
Amaryllis bulbs are not cheap, which is why I like to keep them from year to year. To do this, remove the flowering stems after they've faded and continue to water the bulbs, adding some all-purpose fertilizer every week from spring to summer. The plants can live outside after the frosts in late spring. New foliage will grow from the remaining stems.

When the leaves turn yellow in late summer or early autumn, stop watering and feeding. Allow the foliage to dry out, then cut it back to 5cm (2in) from the top of the bulb. Remove the bulbs or leave them in their pots and move them to a cool, dark place for a minimum of six weeks, before replanting them, as shown here, to bloom again in winter.

FORAGED FOLIAGE AND BRANCHES

If you want an instant pick-me-up for your winter patio, this simple display of cut stems and branches offers colour and texture at no extra cost. Some stems will also root into the compost to make free plants.

If you like foraging for seasonal wreaths, try this quick and easy project with some of the stems and branches you collect. I harvest stems in early winter from evergreens in my garden, including a Mexican orange blossom (*Choisya ternata*), variegated holly (*Ilex*), dogwood (*Cornus sanguinea* 'Midwinter Fire'), and bay (*Laurus nobilis*), which together create a spectacular, eye-catching display to brighten up the gloomy winter months. You could also include conifer branches, if you have some. The red dogwood stems make a statement, but if you don't have these in your garden, try the gnarled branches of deciduous shrubs, bronze-leaved beech (*Fagus*) or hornbeam (*Carpinus*), or any other twiggy growth you have to hand.

You will need
Stems from shrubs in the garden
Secateurs
Peat-free multi-purpose compost
Decorative frost-proof or frost-resistant pot

1. Take a look around your garden or friends' gardens, if they don't mind, for large evergreen shrubs from which you can take a few stems, without spoiling the look of the original plant. Do not remove stems from young plants that are still establishing. Collect some with different coloured stems and leaves and twiggy growth for additional textural interest.

2. Cut the stems just below a leaf joint or node (bump or mark on the stem, from which a new shoot will develop). Fill a large pot with multi-purpose compost and water to moisten it if it is dry.

3. "Plant" the evergreen stems in the compost by simply plunging them in to secure them.

4. Finally, add the longer, colourful dogwood stems or twiggy branches to create drama. Set the pot on a table, chair, or patio where it will catch the winter light. The stems will remain looking fresh for the rest of the season.

Aftercare
This pot will look after itself, although you may have to water the compost during a prolonged dry period, if the stems start to wilt. In late spring, tip the contents out of the pot and remove stems that have rooted. Transfer them to containers of peat-free multi-purpose compost to grow on. Any stems without roots can be added to the compost heap.

Plants for a winter branch display
Hornbeam (*Carpinus*); Mexican orange blossom (*Choisya ternata*); dogwoods (*Cornus*); twisted hazel (*Corylus avellana* 'Contorta'); beech (*Fagus*); bay (*Laurus nobilis*); variegated holly (*Ilex*).

1.

2.

3.

4.

CONTAINER PLANT PROPAGATION GUIDE

This easy-to-use guide shows you the best propagation methods and timings for the container plants in the book, together with some other popular species.

Remember, too, that propagation is not black and white, and these are just guidelines. I always recommend experimenting to see which methods work for you, since the cost is minimal, and you won't lose much by trying.

The propagation techniques are described in more detail on the pages below:

Division: pp.24–5
Hardwood cuttings: pp.26–9
Layering: p.34
Offsets: p.112
Rooting in water: p.29
Seed sowing: pp.30–1
Semi-ripe cuttings: p.26
Softwood cuttings: p.26

PLANT	Propagation method	\multicolumn{12}{c}{Months}
		J	F	M	A	M	J	J	A	S	O	N	D
Acer	hardwood cuttings	■										■	■
	seeds sown directly									■	■		
Achillea	division			■						■			
	Seeds sown under cover		■	■									
Aeonium	offsets	■	■									■	■
	stem cuttings	■	■									■	■
Agapanthus	division			■						■			
	seeds sown under cover			■	■								
Agastache	division			■						■			
	seeds sown under cover		■	■									
Ageratum houstonianum	seeds sown under cover		■	■									
Allium hollandicum	division						■						
Allium schoenoprasum (chives)	division			■						■			
	seeds sown under cover		■		■								
Antirrhinum	seeds sown under cover	■	■										
Aster ageratoides	division			■		■							
	semi-ripe cuttings							■	■				
	softwood cuttings					■							
Aster × frikartii	semi-ripe cuttings							■	■				
	softwood cuttings			■		■							
Astilbe	division			■						■			
	seeds sown under cover			■									
Astrantia major	division			■							■	■	
	seeds sown under cover	■						■					

174 Container Plant Propagation Guide

PLANT	Propagation method	\multicolumn{12}{c}{Months}

PLANT	Propagation method	J	F	M	A	M	J	J	A	S	O	N	D
Aucuba japonica	layering			■	■	■	■	■	■	■	■		
	semi-ripe cuttings							■	■	■			
Bacopa	layering		■	■	■		■		■	■			
	Seeds sown under cover		■	■	■	■							
	softwood cuttings			■	■	■	■	■					
Basil	seeds sown directly				■	■	■	■					
	seeds sown under cover		■	■	■	■	■	■	■				
Begonia	division			■	■					■	■		
	leaf cuttings				■	■	■	■	■				
	Seeds sown under cover	■	■	■	■								
Bergenia	division			■	■					■	■		
	seeds sown directly				■	■	■						
	seeds sown under cover		■	■	■								
Bidens	seeds sown under cover	■	■	■									
Brachyscome	seeds sown under cover	■	■	■	■								
	softwood cuttings				■	■	■						
Briza media	seeds sown directly			■	■	■							
Buddleja	hardwood cuttings	■	■	■							■	■	■
	semi-ripe cuttings								■	■	■		
	softwood cuttings				■	■	■						
Calamintha nepeta	division			■	■					■	■		
	seeds sown under cover	■	■	■						■	■	■	■
	softwood cuttings				■	■							
Calendula (pot marigold)	seeds sown directly			■	■	■							
	seeds sown under cover		■	■	■					■	■		

PLANT	Propagation method	J	F	M	A	M	J	J	A	S	O	N	D
Calluna (heather)	layering			■	■	■							
	seeds sown under cover			■	■	■							
	semi-ripe cuttings							■	■	■			
Camellia	hardwood cuttings	■	■										
	layering				■	■							
	semi-ripe cuttings								■	■			
Campanula lactiflora	seeds sown under cover			■	■								
Campanula poscharskyana	division			■	■					■	■		
	Seeds sown under cover			■	■	■	■						
	softwood cuttings				■	■	■						
Canna	division			■	■								
Carex morrowii	division									■	■		
Ceanothus	semi-ripe cuttings							■	■				
	softwood cuttings				■	■	■						
Cerinthe major	seeds sown directly						■	■					
	seeds sown under cover			■					■	■			
Choisya	semi-ripe cuttings							■	■				
Clematis	layering				■	■							
Cobaea scandens	seeds sown under cover		■	■	■					■	■		
Conifer trees	semi-ripe cuttings								■	■			
	seeds sown directly										■	■	
Coreopsis	softwood cuttings				■	■							
	division			■	■								
	seeds sown under cover		■	■									

Container Plant Propagation Guide

PLANT	Propagation method	\multicolumn{12}{c}{Months}
		J	F	M	A	M	J	J	A	S	O	N	D
Cornus	layering			■	■					■	■	■	
	hardwood cuttings	■	■									■	■
	semi-ripe cuttings								■	■	■		
Corylus avellana 'Contorta'	hardwood cuttings	■	■									■	■
	semi-ripe cuttings							■	■				
Cosmos (annual)	seeds sown directly				■	■							
	seeds sown under cover			■	■								
	softwood cuttings				■	■							
Cosmos atrosanguineus	division		■							■			
	semi-ripe cuttings							■	■				
	softwood cuttings			■	■	■							
Cotinus	hardwood cuttings	■	■									■	■
	layering									■	■		
Crocus	division				■								
Dahlia	division			■									
	softwood cuttings			■	■								
	seeds sown under cover			■	■								
Daphne	hardwood cuttings	■	■									■	■
	semi-ripe cuttings								■	■	■		
Dianthus barbatus (sweet William)	seeds sown directly					■	■						
	seeds sown under cover			■	■								
	softwood cuttings			■	■								
Dianthus (pink)	seeds sown under cover			■	■	■							
	semi-ripe cuttings								■	■	■		
	softwood cuttings			■	■	■							
Echeveria	leaf cuttings	■	■	■	■	■	■	■	■	■	■	■	■

PLANT	Propagation method	J	F	M	A	M	J	J	A	S	O	N	D
Echinacea	division			■	■	■			■	■	■		
	seeds sown under cover		■	■	■	■			■	■			
Erigeron karvinskianus	division			■	■					■	■		
	seeds sown directly				■	■	■						
	seeds sown under cover		■	■	■	■							
	softwood cuttings					■	■	■					
Erysimum cheiri (wallflower)	seeds sown directly								■	■			
	seeds sown under cover	■	■	■	■								■
	softwood cuttings					■	■	■					
Eucalyptus gunnii (dwarf form)	seeds sown directly				■	■				■			
	seeds sown under cover		■	■	■	■	■						
Eucomis bicolor	offsets			■									
	seeds sown under cover	■	■	■	■	■	■	■	■	■	■	■	■
Euonymus fortunei	semi-ripe cuttings							■	■	■	■		
Euphorbia	seeds sown directly				■	■	■						
	seeds sown under cover			■	■	■	■						
Fatsia japonica	seeds sown under cover		■	■	■	■	■	■					
	semi-ripe cuttings						■	■	■				
Festuca glauca	division			■	■								
	seeds sown directly				■	■							
	Seeds sown under cover		■	■	■								
Foeniculum vulgare (fennel)	seeds sown directly				■	■							
Fuchsia	semi-ripe cuttings								■	■	■		
	softwood cuttings			■	■	■							

PLANT	Propagation method	J	F	M	A	M	J	J	A	S	O	N	D
Galanthus (snowdrop)	division		■	■	■								
Gaultheria mucronata	semi-ripe cuttings							■	■	■			
Geranium (cranesbill)	division			■	■					■	■		
Geum	division			■	■					■	■		
Glandora prostrata syn. *Lithodora diffusa*	semi-ripe cuttings							■	■	■			
Hebe	semi-ripe cuttings							■	■	■			
	softwood cuttings			■	■	■							
Hedera helix (ivy)	semi-ripe cuttings							■	■	■			
	softwood cuttings			■	■	■							
Helianthus annuus (sunflower)	seeds sown directly				■								
	seeds sown under cover			■									
Heliotropium	seeds sown under cover		■	■									
Helleborus (hellebore)	division			■									
	seeds sown directly						■						
	seeds sown under cover	■	■	■	■	■	■	■	■	■	■	■	■
Heuchera	division			■	■					■	■		
	seeds sown under cover	■	■	■	■	■	■	■	■	■	■	■	■
Hosta	division			■	■	■							
Hyacinthus	division						■						
Hydrangea	hardwood cuttings	■	■									■	■
	semi-ripe cuttings								■	■	■		
	softwood cuttings			■	■	■							
Hippeastrum	offsets	■	■										
Ipomoea	seeds sown directly					■	■						
	seeds sown under cover		■	■	■								

PLANT	Propagation method	J	F	M	A	M	J	J	A	S	O	N	D
Iris reticulata	division			■	■								
Jasminum	layering			■	■	■	■						
	semi-ripe cuttings							■	■	■			
Kalanchoe thyrsiflora	leaf cuttings			■	■	■	■		■				
	offsets	■	■	■	■	■	■	■	■	■	■	■	■
Lamium maculatum	division			■	■					■	■		
Lathyrus odoratus (sweet pea)	seeds sown directly				■	■							
	seeds sown under cover		■	■						■	■		
	softwood cuttings				■	■	■						
Lavandula (lavender)	hardwood cuttings	■	■								■	■	
	semi-ripe cuttings							■	■	■			
	softwood cuttings			■	■	■	■						
Leucojum	division					■	■						
Limonium vulgare	seeds sown under cover		■	■									
Lobelia	division			■	■								
	seeds sown under cover		■	■	■								
	softwood cuttings				■	■	■						
Lomandra 'White Sands'	division				■					■	■		
	seeds sown under cover			■	■								
Lonicera (honeysuckle)	seeds sown under cover		■	■	■								
	semi-ripe cuttings							■	■	■			
	softwood cuttings			■	■	■	■						
Lysimachia atropurpurea	division			■	■					■	■		
Lysimachia nummularia	division			■	■					■	■		
	seeds sown under cover		■	■	■					■	■		
	softwood cuttings				■	■	■		■				

PLANT	Propagation method	J	F	M	A	M	J	J	A	S	O	N	D
Magnolia stellata	layering			■	■	■							
	semi-ripe cuttings							■	■	■			
Mentha (mint)	division			■	■					■	■	■	
	softwood cuttings				■	■	■						
Miscanthus sinensis (dwarf form)	division			■	■								
	seeds sown under cover		■	■									
Muehlenbeckia	division			■	■								
	softwood cuttings					■	■	■	■				
Muscari	division							■	■				
Myosotis sylvatica (forget-me-not)	seeds sown directly					■	■						
	seeds sown under cover						■	■					
Narcissus	division						■						
Nemesia	seeds sown under cover		■	■	■	■							
	softwood cuttings				■	■	■						
Nepeta	division			■	■					■	■		
	semi-ripe cuttings								■	■			
	softwood cuttings				■	■							
Nerine	division					■	■						
Nicotiana	seeds sown under cover			■									
Oenothera lindheimeri (gaura)	seeds sown under cover	■	■	■									
	semi-ripe cuttings								■	■			
	softwood cuttings			■	■								
Ophiopogon planiscapus	division			■	■	■							

PLANT	Propagation method	J	F	M	A	M	J	J	A	S	O	N	D
Origanum vulgare (oregano)	division			■	■					■	■		
	seeds sown under cover		■	■	■								
	softwood cuttings				■	■	■						
Osmanthus heterophyllus	semi-ripe cuttings							■	■	■			
Osteospermum	seeds sown under cover		■	■									
	semi-ripe cuttings								■	■			
	softwood cuttings					■	■	■					
Panicum virgatum	division				■	■							
	seeds sown under cover			■	■								
Passiflora caerulea	layering								■	■	■		
	seeds sown under cover			■	■	■							
	semi-ripe cuttings							■	■				
Pelargonium	seeds sown under cover	■	■										
	semi-ripe cuttings								■	■			
	softwood cuttings			■	■	■							
Pennisetum	division				■	■							
Penstemon	seeds sown under cover		■	■				■	■				
	semi-ripe cuttings							■	■				
Petunia	softwood cuttings			■	■	■							
Phlox drummondii	seeds sown under cover		■	■									
Phlox paniculata	seeds sown under cover	■	■								■	■	■
	semi-ripe cuttings								■	■			
	softwood cuttings			■	■	■							
Physocarpus opulifolius	semi-ripe cuttings							■	■				
	softwood cuttings			■	■	■	■						

PLANT	Propagation method	J	F	M	A	M	J	J	A	S	O	N	D
Pieris	semi-ripe cuttings							■	■	■			
	softwood cuttings			■	■	■							
Pittosporum	layering			■	■								
	semi-ripe cuttings								■	■	■		
Platycodon grandiflorus	seeds sown directly					■	■						
	seeds sown under cover			■	■								
	softwood cuttings				■	■							
Primula	division			■	■								
	seeds sown under cover			■	■	■	■		■	■	■		
Rhodochiton atrosanguineus	layering				■	■							
	semi-ripe cuttings							■	■				
Rose	hardwood cuttings	■										■	■
	semi-ripe cuttings								■	■	■		
	softwood cuttings				■	■	■						
Rudbeckia	division			■	■								
	seeds sown directly				■	■							
	seeds sown under cover		■	■	■								
Salvia	division			■	■	■							
	seeds sown under cover		■	■	■	■	■		■	■	■		
	semi-ripe cuttings								■	■			
	softwood cuttings				■	■	■						
Salvia rosmarinus (rosemary)	seeds sown under cover			■	■								
	semi-ripe cuttings								■	■			
	softwood cuttings				■	■							
Sambucus nigra f. *porphyrophylla*	semi-ripe cuttings								■	■			
	softwood cuttings				■	■							
Sarcococca	semi-ripe cuttings								■	■	■		
	softwood cuttings				■	■	■						

PLANT	Propagation method	J	F	M	A	M	J	J	A	S	O	N	D
Saxifraga	division			X	X	X	X						
	seeds sown under cover		X	X	X	X	X	X	X	X			
Scabiosa incisa	division			X									
	seeds sown under cover			X									
Sedum album	division			X	X								
	softwood cuttings			X	X	X	X						
Sempervivum	offsets				X	X	X		X				
Setaria	seeds sown directly				X	X							
	seeds sown under cover		X	X	X								
Scilla forbesii	division						X						
Skimmia	semi-ripe cuttings								X	X	X		
	softwood cuttings			X	X	X	X						
Solenostemon	seeds sown under cover			X	X								
	softwood cuttings			X	X	X	X						
	semi-ripe cuttings							X	X				
Stipa lessingiana	division			X	X								
	seeds sown under cover	X	X	X									
Stipa tenuissima	division			X	X								
	seeds sown under cover		X	X	X							X	X
Symphyotrichum (aster)	division			X	X								
	semi-ripe cuttings								X	X			
	softwood cuttings			X	X	X	X						
Syringa vulgaris (lilac)	hardwood cuttings	X										X	X
	semi-ripe cuttings									X	X		
Tagetes (French marigold)	seeds sown directly					X							
	seeds sown under cover		X	X	X								

PLANT	Propagation method	J	F	M	A	M	J	J	A	S	O	N	D
Thunbergia alata	seeds sown under cover	■	■									■	■
Thymus (thyme)	division			■	■								
	seeds sown directly			■	■	■				■	■	■	
	seeds sown under cover		■	■	■								
Tiarella	division			■	■					■	■		
	seeds sown under cover			■	■					■	■		
Tropaeolum majus (nasturtium)	seeds sown directly				■	■	■						
	seeds sown under cover			■	■								
Tulipa clusiana	division								■	■			
Verbena bonariensis	seeds sown directly					■	■						
	seeds sown under cover			■	■								
	semi-ripe cuttings								■	■	■		
	softwood cuttings			■	■								
Viburnum	layering						■	■					
	semi-ripe cuttings								■	■	■		
	softwood cuttings			■	■								
Viola	seeds sown under cover		■	■						■	■		
	seeds sown directly			■	■					■	■		
Zinnia	seeds sown directly			■	■								
	seeds sown under cover			■	■								
	softwood cuttings			■	■								

RESOURCES

Other books from Anya
You may find my two previous books useful.

The Money-Saving Garden Year **by Anya Lautenbach (DK, 2024)**
This invaluable book is packed with ideas for each month of the year to keep your garden looking beautiful on a budget.

The Money-Saving Gardener **by Anya Lautenbach (DK, 2024)**
My practical gardening guide, offering a wealth of tips and tricks for creating a low-cost garden, brimming with gorgeous plants.

Recommended books
The following books are great resources for any money-conscious gardener. They are all well worth buying, or you could see if your local library has copies to borrow.

RHS A–Z Encyclopedia of Garden Plants **edited by Christopher Brickell, 4th edition (DK, 2016)**
This truly is my bible. The most reliable source of information about garden plants.

RHS Propagating Plants **edited by Alan Toogood (DK, 2019)**
This book is a must-have for anyone who would like to understand more about propagation, featuring over 1,500 different plants.

RHS Pruning and Training **by Christopher Brickell and David Joyce (DK, 2017)**
Everything you need to know about pruning over 800 plants.

Websites

Butterfly Conservation
butterfly-conservation.org
A resource for learning, identifying, and understanding the most wonderful butterflies and moths, with ideas on how to provide what they need in your pots and wider garden.

Coppice Products
coppice-products.co.uk
This is a directory of coppice product makers in the UK, useful for finding wood for creating plant supports.

Pinterest
pinterest.co.uk
I often use Pinterest in the winter just to feed my mind with ideas. It's a great place for money-saving gardeners who are looking for inspiration.

Royal Horticultural Society (RHS)
rhs.org.uk
There is no better place for me when looking for advice than the RHS website. Always up to date, it includes everything you need.

The Wildlife Trusts
wildlifetrusts.org
A great source of information on how to make the pots and containers in your garden more wildlife friendly.

INDEX

Note: page numbers in **bold** refer to images and information contained in captions.

A
acer 79
achillea 71, 102
acid-loving plants 34, 41, 52, 57, **78**, 79, 85, 127
 see also ericaceous plants
aeonium **114**, 115, 131
agapanthus 13, 17, **92**, 92, 101, 116, 132, 159
Ageratum 102, **103**
alkaline conditions 34
allium 65, **65**, 106, 131
amaryllis (*Hippeastrum*) 6, 155, **155**, **168**, 169
Ammi majus 102
angel hair grass (*Stipa*) 128, **128**, 152
annuals 37, 49, 159
 autumnal 126, 139, 144
 climbers 42, **60**, 61
 compost for 52
 deadheading 98
 feeding 57
 fragrant 45
 sowing 30, 71–2, 90, 97
 summer 91, 93, 97, 98, 102, 106, **107**
 for year-round interest 37
aquilegia 33
architectural plants 34
aster 37, 61, 124–5, **124**, 152, 155
astrantia 33, 46, 116, 132
Aucuba japonica 46
auricula 82, **83**
autumn 123–48
autumn-to-spring pots **146**, 147
azalea 34, 45, 52, 79

B
baby's breath 102, **103**
bacopa (*Chaenostoma*) 49, 106
balconies, load-bearing 21
bare-root plants 85, 116
basil 144, 159
bay (*Laurus nobilis*) 46, 170

beans 6
bedding plants 13, 21, 57, 101
beech (*Fagus*) 170
begonia 21, 29, 49, 72
bergenia 46
berries 17
biennials 33, 67
biodegradable materials 10, 13
birch (*Betula*) 61
black-eyed Susan (*Thunbergia*) 42, **43**, 61, 132
blueberry **40**, 41, 79
bowden lily (*Nerine*) 127
bulbs 23, 25, 72
 bulb lasagnes 131
 festive 157
 see also spring bulbs
bunny tails (*Lagurus ovatus*) 132
busy lizzies (*Impatiens*) 46

C
camellias 34, 46, 52, 57, **78**, 79
capillary matting 75–6
catmint (*Nepeta*) 25, **93**, 93, 101, 116, **130**, 132
Cerinthe **32**, 71, 102, 132
chalk 34
chillies 41
chionodoxa (*Scilla*) 66, **66**
chives **64**, 65
Christmas 17, 45, **130**, 132, 157
Christmas trees, from seed 162, **163**
clematis 42, **43**, 61
climbers 26, **40**, 42, **43**
 beans 6
 cucamelons **118**, 119
 layering 34
 support for 42, **43**, **60**, 61
 see also specific climbers
cloud grass (*Agrostis nebulosa*) 102
colanders 112, **113**
coleus 71, 91, **91**
colour 16, 17, 46
comfrey fertilizer **56**, 57
compost 52–3, **53**
concrete pots 14
coneflowers 37, 71, 90, **90**
 see also Echinacea
conifers 17

container "feet" 21, 58, **59**
container gardens, creating 9–21
containers
 care for 51–61
 choice of 10–14
 cleaning 13
 colour 17, 46
 DIY 13
 materials 14
 reusing 10–13, **12**
 shape 13–14
 siting 21
 size of 13
 upcycled 10–13, **12**
 weight 21
copper shield fern (*Dryopteris*) 46
coriander 46
cosmos 21, 30, 71, **90**, 91, 102
cottage gardens 17
courgette 41
crocus 25, 66–7, **67**, 71, 131
cucamelon 41, **118**, 119
cucumber **40**
cup and saucer vine (*Cobaea*) 61, 132
currants 41
cut flowers 102, **103**
cut-and-come-again crops 46
cuttings 23, 26–9, **28**, **70**
 basal 29
 dahlia **27**, 29, 72, **73**, 92
 hardwood 26–9, **27**, 111, 159
 ivy 152, **152**
 lavender 72, 94, **100**, 101
 leaf **27**, 29, 148, **149**
 overwintering **48**, 49, 106, 131
 pansies 147
 roses 111
 salvia 97
 semi-ripe 26, 94, 101, **130**, 132, 154
 snail trails **74**, 75
 softwood 26, **27**, 72, 92, 101
 succulents 115
 taken in autumn 132, **133**
 taken in summer 101
 in water 29, 72, 159
cyclamen 139

Index **187**

D

daffodil (*Narcissus*) 25, 64, **68**, 71, 147
  deadheading **73**
  paperwhites 60, 69, 132, 160, **161**
  planting 131, 132
  shade-loving 46
  'Thalia' 45
dahlia 92, **93**
  cuttings **27**, 29, 72, **73**, 92
  overwintering 49
  planting 72
  seeds 71, 132
daphne 45
deadheading 72, **73**, 98, **99**
delphinium 71
design 16–17
diascia 49
Dichondra **12**
dill 144
  florist's 102
division 25, **25**, 72
  auricula 82, **83**
  grasses 128
  hostas 86, **87**
  spring bulbs 25
  summer 101
dogwood (*Cornus*) 170
drainage 10, 58, **59**
drought-tolerant plants **12**, 13, 14, 52, 67, 97, 112, 127, 142, 144, 159
drying plants 144, **145**

E

Echeveria 37, 72
Echinacea 37, 71, 90, **90**, 152, 155
ericaceous plants 34, **40**, **53**, **78**, 79, 105, 127, 153
  see also acid-loving plants
Euonymus 154–5, **154**
evergreens 67, 91, 94, 97, 106, 139, 147, 152, 159
  ferns 152
  grasses 15, 37, 125, 128, **129**
  perennials 85, 91, 155, 157
  shade-loving **138**, 139
  shrubs 34, 37, **78**, 79, 127, **127**, 132, **133**, 152–5, **154**, 170

F

Fatsia 154
feeding plants **56**, 57, 101, 132
fences 46
ferns 46, 152
fertilizer **56**, 57, 69, 72, 101, 132
Festuca 37, 128
flowering season, extension 45
foam flower (*Tiarella*) 37, **47**, 67, **67**
foliage, foraged 170, **171**
forget-me-not (*Myosotis*) **32**, 33, 67, **146**, 147
fortune's spindle (*Euonymus fortunei*) 154–5, **154**
fountain grass (*Pennisetum*) 125–6, **125**, 128
foxglove (*Digitalis*) 33
foxtail millet (*Setaria*) 37
fragrance **44**, 45
French marigold (*Tagetes*) 21, 30
fritillary 159
front doors 16, **25**
frost 14, 30, 37, 41, 49, 144
fruit 17, **40**, 41, 46, **118**, 119–21, **120**
  bushes 26, 29
  see also specific fruit
fuchsia 21, 34, **35**, 46, 92–3, 101, 132
fungal diseases 58

G

gaura (*Oenothera*) 33, 61, 71, 92, **92**, 101, 106
geranium
  hardy **32**, 33, 116
  see also pelargonium
germination 30
grape hyacinth (*Muscari*) 25, 64–5, **64**, 131, 132
grasses *see* ornamental grasses

H

half-hardy plants 30, 49, 72, 98
hanging baskets 14, 21, **40**, 112
hardy plants 30, 49, 72, 85, 131
hazel (*Corylus*) 61
  twisted 170
heather (*Calluna*) 79, 127, **127**
  winter-flowering (*Erica*) 34
hebe 21, 34, **35**, 127, **127**
heliotropes 45, 71
hellebore 21, 152, **156**, 157
hellebore leaf spot 157

herbs 17, 34, 67, 97–8
  cuttings 26, 72, 101, 159
  dividing 25
  shade-loving 46
  storage 144, **145**
  see also specific herbs
heuchera (coral bells) 37, 46, 116, **125**, 125, 139
holiday care 76, 101
holly (*Ilex*), variegated 170
holly olive (*Osmanthus*) 46
honeysuckle (*Lonicera*) 61
honeywort (*Cerinthe*) **32**, 71
hornbeam (*Carpinus*) 170
horticultural grit 52–3, **53**
hosta 25, **47**, 86, **87**, 116
houseleek (*Sempervivum*) 13, 37, 72, 112, **130**, 131
houseleek tree **114**, 115, 131
houseplants **27**, 29, 52–3
hyacinth **44**, 45, 60, 65–6, **65**, 71, **130**, 131–2
hydrangea **35**, 37, 46, 72
  blue-flowered 34, 105
  propagation **104**, 105
  seedheads 155, **155**

I, J, K

Ipomoea batatas 42
iris 71, 131
ivy (*Hedera*) 17, 37, 42, 46, 139, 152–3, **152**
Japanese aralia (*Fatsia*) 154
Japanese maple (*Acer palmatum*) 79
jasmine 61
John Innes formulas 52–3, **53**
jonquils 45, 69
kohlrabi 41, **136**, 137

L

large plants 13–14, 21, 42, **43**
larkspur (*Consolida ajacis*) 71
lavender 17, 72, **95**, 132, 159
  caring for 94
  choosing 94
  cutting back **99**
  fragrance 45
  how to grow 94
  overwintering 159
  propagation 33, 72, 94, **95**, **100**, 101, 132
  siting 21

layering 34
leaf mould 53
Lenten rose (*Helleborus*) 157
lettuce 41, 46
Leucanthemum **70**
light levels 21
lily 72
  Asiatic 72
Lomandra **84**, 85
long-flowering displays 106, **107**
love-in-a-mist (*Nigella*) 132
lupin 71

M
mallow **32**
marigold 17, 71, 132
  see also French marigold
Mediterranean plants 17
metal containers 14, 21
Mexican fleabane (*Erigeron*) 33, **36**, 37, 71, 101, 142, **143**
Mexican orange blossom (*Choisya*) 170
mibuna 46
microgreens **158**, 159
mildew, powdery 58
mint 25, 26, 46, 144, 159
Miscanthus 37, 155, 159
mizuna 46
mondo grass (*Ophiopogon*) 155
morning glory (*Ipomoea*) 71
Muehlenbeckia **114**, 115
mulching 54–5, **55**, 98

N, O
nasturtium (*Tropaeolum*) 30, 71
necklace vine (*Muehlenbeckia*) 115, 139
Nemesia 45, 49, 93, 131
netting 30
nettles 57
offsets 25, 72, 112
orchids 52–3
oregano 26
ornamental grasses **129**, 132, 152
  aftercare 128
  choosing 129
  cutting back 159
  evergreen 37, 125, 128
  planting 128
  propagation 25, **25**, 33, 128
  see also specific grasses
overwintering 30, **48**, 49, 106, 131–2

P
paddle plant (*Kalanchoe*) 37, 131, 148, **149**
painted nettle 71, 91, **91**
Panicum 37
pansy (*Viola*) 71, 101, 126, **126**, 132, 139, **146**, 147
parsley 46, 144
peat 52
pelargoniums **48**, 49, 101, 132
peony (*Paeonia*) 101, 116, **117**
peppers 41
perennials 23, 72, 155, 157
  for autumn 124–5, 142
  bare-root 116
  buying 72
  climbers 42
  compost for 52–3
  deadheading 98
  evergreen 85, 91, 155, 157
  feeding 57, 71
  large 13–14
  long-lasting shrub and perennial medley **84**, 85
  overwintering 49
  propagation 25, 29, 30, 33, 71–2, 101, 132
  repotting 71
  shade-loving **47**
  for spring 66–7, **67**
  for summer 90–3, **92**, 97, 102, 106
  supports for **60**, 61
  for year-round interest 37
  see also specific perennials
petunia 21, 30, 45
Phacelia 102
phlox, border 61
Pieris 34, 79
pinks (*Dianthus*) 45, 91, **91**
Pittosporum 34, **84**, 85, **133**
Plant Breeders Rights 111
plant protection 30, 58, **59**
  see also overwintering
plant support 42, 60–1, **60**
plastic containers 10, 14, 21
plug plants **70**, 72
Polypodium vulgare 46
poppy, opium 132
potager displays 17
potato 41
primrose 66

primula 25, 46, 66, 101
  see also auricula
propagation 23, 25–30, **25**, **27–8**, **31**
  in autumn 101
  grasses 25, **25**, 33, 128
  hydrangea **104**, 105
  lavender 33, 72, 94, **95**, **100**, 101, 132
  shrubs 26, **27**, 34, 72
  snail trails **74**, 75–6, **77**
  succulents **27**, 29, 72, 115, 148, **149**
  sweet peas 30, 42, **43**, 76, 132, 134, **135**
  see also cuttings; division; seeds
pruning 159
prunings 42
purple bell vine (*Rhodochiton*) 42, 61

R
rainwater harvesting 54, 98
repotting plants 71
rhododendron 34, 46, 52, 57, 79
root-bound plants 71
roots 13, 54, 58
roses 17, 26, 45, 58, **110**, 111, 159
  cuttings 26, **27**
  pruning 159
rosemary (*Salvia rosmarinus*) 21, **66**, 67, 101, 159
Rudbeckia 37

S
salad leaves 41, 46
salvia 17, 33, 34, 49, 71, 97, 101, 116, 132, **145**, 159
  Salvia viridis 102, **103**
  Salvia 'Amethyst Lips' 106
  Salvia 'Amistad' **96**, 97, 101
  see also rosemary
Saxifraga × *arendsii* 67, **67**
second-hand containers 10, **10**, **14**
sedge (*Carex*) 25, **25**, **36**, 37, 128, **129**, 132, 139
  Japanese 128, 153, **153**
sedum 13, 37, 112, 131
seed pots, paper **12**, 13, **14**
seedheads 37, 152, 155, **155**
seedlings
  collecting self-sown 33
  forget-me-not 147
  kohlrabi 137
  Mexican fleabane (*Erigeron*) 142

sweet pea 134, **135**
transplanting 30, 41, 76, **146**
seeds 23, 30, **31**, 41, 65, 71–3
   Christmas tree 162, **163**
   climbers 42, **43**, 119
   collection **130**, 132
   kohlrabi 137
   Mexican fleabane (*Erigeron*) 142
   microgreens **158**, 159
   overwintering 132
   self-seeding plants **32**, 33, 157
   to sow in summer 101, 119
self-seeding plants **32**, 33, 157
shade-loving plants 46, **47**, **138**, 139
shrubs 13–14, 21, 23, 34, **35**, 46, 52,
   57, 71
   dioecious 153
   evergreen 34, 37, **78**, 79, **127**, 127, 132, **133**, 152–5, **154**, 170
   long-lasting shrub and perennial medley **84**, 85
   propagation 26, **27**, 34, 72
   see also specific shrubs
silver nickel vine (*Dichondra argentea*) 106
silverbush (*Convolvulus cneorum*) 106
skimmia 34, 52, **84**, 85, 152, **152**, 153
slugs and snails 41, 76, 86, 101
smoke bush (*Cotinus*) 126, **126**
snail trails **28**, **74**, 75–6, **77**
snapdragon (*Antirrhinum*) 49, 131
sneezeweed (*Helenium*) 124, **124**
snowdrop (*Galanthus*) 25, 46, 152, 164, **165**–7
soft shield fern (*Polystichum*) 46, 152
soil block makers 13, **70**
soil residue marks 21
spring 63–86
spring bulbs 13, 25, 58, 60, 64–7, 69, 71, 72, **73**, 131, 159
spring snowflake (*Leucojum*) 159
spurge (*Euphorbia*) 147, 152, 154, **154**
squirrels 58
statice (*Limonium*) 102
Stipa 128, **128**, 152, 155, 159
stocks (*Matthiola*) 45

stone containers 14
strawberries **40**, 41, 46, 120–1, **120**
strawflowers (*Helichrysum*) 102
style 17
succulents 131
   compost for 53
   overwintering 159
   pot size 13, **20**
   potting ideas 112, **113–14**, 115
   propagation **27**, 29, 72, 115, 148, **149**
   for year-round interest **36**, 37
summer 89–121
summer bedding plants 13, 21, 57
summer bulbs 72
sun-loving plants **20**, 21, 144
   see also drought-resistant plants
sunflower (*Helianthus*) 30
surfaces 21
sweet alyssum (*Lobularia*) 45
sweet box (*Sarcococca*) 34, **35**, 45, 152, 153–4, **153**
sweet pea (*Lathyrus*) 17, 45, 71, 132
   extending the flowering season 61
   fragrance 45
   planting ideas 134, **135**
   pot size 13
   propagation 30, 42, **43**, 76, 132, 134, **135**
   supporting **60**, 61
sweet rocket (*Hesperis*) 132
sweet William (*Dianthus*) 45

T
tender plants 49, 72, 76, 126
   annuals 30, 144
   climbers 42
   planting out 98
   see also overwintering
terracotta pots 10, **10**, 13, 14, **64**, 155
   "frostproof" 14
themes 17
"thriller, filler, spiller" principle 16–7
thyme 25, 26, 34, 144, **145**
Tiarella 37, **47**, 67, **67**
tobacco plants (*Nicotiana*) 45, 46, 102, **103**
tomatoes **40**, 41

trailing plants 17, 42, **66**, 67, 106, **107**, 119, 139, 152
trees 13–4, 17, 21, 52, 71
tufted hairgrass (*Deschampsia*) 37, 128
tulip 71, 131

V
vegetables 17, **40**, 41, 46, **118**, 119, **136**, 137
verbena 33, 132
   Verbena bonariensis **32**, 33, 93
   Verbena rigida 102, **103**
Viburnum 45, 46, 101
viola 46, 101, 132

W
wall wires 42, 61
wallflower (*Erysimum*) 33, 65, **65**
watering 54–5, **55**, 98, **99**
   hanging baskets 14
   holidays 101
   moisture retention 34, 54–5, **55**
   and siting pots 21
   snail trails 75, 76
wigwams 42
winter 151–70
wooden containers 10, 14, 17, 42, 142, **143**
wreaths, seasonal 170

Y, Z
year-round interest **36**, 37
zinnias 30, 71, 76, 102

Author acknowledgments

I dedicate this book to my followers. I would like you to know what a special place you have in my heart and how much I appreciate your kindness. My books became my wings, allowing me to fly high, and this is only possible because of your support. I hope this book will be helpful and it will become another way for us to connect.

I would like to thank my boys Richard, William, and Edward. You are my everything and I love you more than words can say.

A very big thank you to my Editorial Director at DK, Ruth O'Rourke, whose vision, expertise, and support empowers me. Ruth, you are truly amazing!

My very grateful thanks goes to the wonderful editors Lucy Philpott and Zia Allaway, photographer Britt Willoughby, book designers Barbara Zuniga and Izzy Poulson, and the most incredible team at DK: Maxine Pedliham, Hayley Reed, and Silvia Dembner. It's a privilege for me to work with you all. Your dedication and passion for books inspires me everyday.

Love, Anya xxx

Publisher acknowledgments

DK would like to thank Adam Brackenbury for repro work, Katie Hewett for proofreading, and Lisa Footitt for compiling the index.

Editorial Director Ruth O'Rourke
Project Editor Lucy Philpott
Gardening Design Manager Barbara Zuniga
Design Assistant Izzy Poulson
Production Editor David Almond
Senior Production Controller Stephanie McConnell
DTP and Design Coordinator Heather Blagden
Art Director Maxine Pedliham
Publishing Director Stephanie Jackson

Editorial Zia Allaway
Photography Britt Willoughby

First published in Great Britain in 2026 by
Dorling Kindersley Limited
DK, 20 Vauxhall Bridge Road,
London SW1V 2SA

The authorised representative in the EEA is
Dorling Kindersley Verlag GmbH. Arnulfstr. 124,
80636 Munich, Germany

Copyright © 2026 Dorling Kindersley Limited
Text copyright © Anya Lautenbach 2026

Anya Lautenbach has asserted her right to be identified as the author of this work.

A Penguin Random House Company
10 9 8 7 6 5 4 3 2 1
001–348764–Jan/2026

All rights reserved.

No part of this publication may be reproduced, stored in or introduced into a retrieval system, or transmitted, in any form, or by any means (electronic, mechanical, photocopying, recording, or otherwise), without the prior written permission of the copyright owner.

No part of this publication may be used or reproduced in any manner for the purpose of training artificial intelligence technologies or systems. In accordance with Article 4(3) of the DSM Directive 2019/790, DK expressly reserves this work from the text and data mining exception.

A CIP catalogue record for this book is available from the British Library.

ISBN: 978-0-2417-3307-3

Printed and bound in Italy
www.dk.com

This book was made with Forest Stewardship Council™ certified paper - one small step in DK's commitment to a sustainable future. Learn more at **www.dk.com/uk/information/sustainability**

Anya Lautenbach is a self-taught gardener with a passion for the environment and championing neurodiversity. She is also a *Sunday Times* and *Irish Times* chart-topping author with her first two books: *The Money-Saving Gardener* and *The Money-Saving Garden Year*.

She grew up in Poland, and after travelling for many years in Germany and the Scottish Highlands, she now lives with her husband and two sons in Buckinghamshire, UK, where her garden has blossomed through years of propagation and clever gardening tricks.

Anya's lifelong passion for nature and for propagating plants inspired her to share her knowledge to her followers across social media. There, as Anya the Garden Fairy, she provides easy-to-follow tutorials covering a range of accessible and achievable gardening techniques, and reveals tips and tricks for creating high-impact, low-cost gardens that work in harmony with nature. Anya also uses her platform to raise awareness about neurodiversity and the positive influence that horticulture can have on mental health. She proves that gardening does not need expensive equipment or specialist training – anyone can transform their garden and create something truly amazing.

You can find Anya online at:
    Instagram: @anya_thegarden_fairy
    Facebook: @anya_thegarden_fairy
    TikTok: @anyathegardenfairy
    YouTube: @anyathegardenfairy
    Website: www.anyalautenbach.com